Chillin In A Straightcoat

Based On The Life Of A God
Blessed Schizophrenic

By Robert E Pace

PAGE PUBLISHING
Conneaut Lake, PA

First originally published by Page Publishing 2024

*Names have been changed to protect individuals'
dignity and prevent harassment.*

ISBN 979-8-89315-037-7 (pbk)
ISBN 979-8-89315-055-1 (digital)

Printed in the United States of America

Preface

I always felt like I was being picked at like bugs were on me, like something was just so pesky, always wanting to touch or pick at me.

While recovering from a so-called mental breakdown, I had a strong illusion of me being in a garden as a tree rooted to the ground. I mean, there was an actual picture of me as the tree trunk and bugs with human faces—some in small human form—crawling on me. I would quickly switch energy to either prayer, hate, or use concentration as power to kill or erase my illusions or hallucinations. I always had to switch my energy to protect me from doing something petty or violent.

Having control of myself always was compromised with consequences that were not the norm and were considered immoral or illegal to me and by many others. I knew others wanted to help me but, in many ways, couldn't. Later I kept the feeling that I didn't want too much help from highly considered friends. I began to resent that choice but, at the same time, honoring and cherishing my decision.

Being labeled a schizophrenic and the definition of schizophrenia as an unknown thing. In my opinion, it is a compromise to a greater concept of different techniques, ideas, morals, agendas, corruptions, and other misunderstandings. Having to go to a psych. doctors, therapist, or case manager whose only concern is if you are a threat to hurting others, filling you up with drugs that affect you negatively health-wise—physically, mentally, generationally, economically, and socially—is a cruel and unusual punishment. It can be said that a chemical imbalance or *slip* or synapse malfunction or deterioration in the body's systems is an inherited, gained, learned blessing or gift. Being different or mutated on an upscale or downscale is and should be considered with concern but not labeled negatively as it has been.

In today's society, which has come a long way in the treatment of so-called mental disorders, has stopped or slowed down violent crimes, but most violent crimes and mass violent incidents have been committed by "regular" persons who have been said by the media to need mental help services to promote money agendas and to keep prescribed harmful drugs that have high side effects that are dangerous to the human sexual identity, causing "drone-like" behavior or "doped-up" stagnant behavior to control attitude or aggression. The person sitting in the corner of the room, talking to themselves or are quiet, are not the perps of the school shootings, mall shootings, church and temple shootings, bombings, and the like. The ones that fit the profile of "normal" persons in society have been the culprits.

Is a person tainted, having spoiled blood or bloodline that needs to be erased because they are deemed violent, untrustworthy, socially not fitting into plans, or a threat to someone else or a group of people who have done wrong to them at a certain time or vice versa? In my experiences, a different determination of my diagnosis can be derived from my history, strength, faith, and services of kindness to the community and society. I have done good and bad in this world. I have taken and given love, pain, fear, lies, violence, concern, and care.

Here is my story, spiritually, medically, socially, morally, and visually remembered in written format.

Chapter 1

Early Hood Years

I always felt special or gifted like a motherfucker, like people really couldn't fuck with me. Even back in the days when I wore the fats, the buds, and bells as one of the older homeboys from my hood had ranked on me about. The fats were the fat boy shoestrings. The non-hype name brand shoes were called buddies, and the bells were the bell-bottom jeans. All I could think to say was "These ponys," but never did. I wanted to say something, but he was slightly older. I guess I should have valued his opinion. All I knew was that I really didn't have any problems with my clothes or eating or housing. My family was not rich, but both my parents had good jobs and birthdays and Christmases were great times. I didn't feel he, or any other of the hood friends, really impressed me with playing the dozens or ranking or anything for real, but I did like to see them act and talk in the regular about things we all did from day-to-day in the neighborhood.

I got beat up in the hood around four times and mugged in the back of the head once, but the mug in the back of the head wasn't until later years when I dared a homeboy at the time to sneak up on me while arguing, and I turned around on him, provoking him.

One time, my friends and I were boxing with gloves on at an early preteen age 'cause the police athletic league—known as Pal 5 in the area—was a big thing for us along with Little League Football and CYO Basketball. This particular time, I got mad, like superheated mad, 'cause I was receiving hands real tough from Hank, a hood friend who lived four houses down. I threw the gloves off to the ground and raced at a couple of the homies that were in the way who were watching and cheering for me to get tagged. I raced at them and just started swinging. They thought it was funny. It seemed as though it was always others cheering or wanting me to get beaten up, some even helping. That changed in later years with the hood. It changed to those same people not wanting to take a loss 'cause I was from where they were from. We had a common function of upholding a sense of honor and pride for being from the same area, but that would only be in later years.

One time, an older hood homie whom later I began to cherish helped me get beaten up. I thought it was because I started judo class, that maybe he thought I was thinking I was better or tougher than the other kids in my age group. He grabbed my homeboy Sam, who I was about to fight, and helped him swing on me by grabbing his arms by the forearm and contacting blows for him. He was landing blows on me, and I had to grab him and wrestle him to the ground. Even then I wasn't given recognition and cheered on to win. They wanted me to lose and have a name or a label of a stepping stone or something, I guess. The other two times I can't say I got handled because they were quick incidents; a couple hits to my face or a quick punch and it was over. One time over a Go-Bot action toy.

After that, I felt I needed to fight again after wanting to cry on my father's porch. I wanted to provoke a fight by waiting on the response of me asking for forgiveness for causing trouble over a toy from Hank. He was a hood friend who I always fought with. One time, he threw a football in my face while we were playing catch on the street. I walked down to the house, and I kept hearing and seeing illusions. It was like moving energy going past me down the street as high as the second story of the two family houses in the hood. The illusions had the color of red and gold. As I kept walking, getting more and more nearer to Hank's family house, the color was starting to change to blue, white, gray, and black, then a li'l brightness of the sun appeared. I heard a voice from the sky near the trees that were across the street in front of Hank's family house and farther down, saying, "Here he come and he yellow!" I squinted my eyes with anger, and I saw something drop as if something had fumbled and heard the same voice from sky again say, "Oops, I mean he gold!"

When I got to Hank's family house, his mother came to the door, and being a responsible parent, she said "You two shouldn't be fighting. You are from the same community and neighborhood." As I sat there and waited for Hank to come outside, I saw my energy leaving, but I felt like a fuck nigga. I felt good when I thought I was going to fight. It would have gotten the edge off of me. I knew that if I had started a fight that I would know exactly how to keep my placement in the hood. I was either going to disrespect them fully or continue to let things slide as not being a big deal.

Even after his mother said what she said, I agreed with it and felt a little relieved. It was internally still too quick of an agreement to me. I guess my energy was too strong to just relinquish without more being said or done. I then felt the need, the urge, to swing on him when he came outside. I felt like a fuck nigga. I was standing there, sizing him up to sneak on him, getting closer and closer, and trying to stand at an angle to get at least one perfect strike. His older brother saw me conniving, and his grandmother yelled from the top porch, "You best not hit him!" I felt good! It felt good that they knew about me like that. Even though I didn't get a chance to, it was still recognized.

I don't remember what happened after that. All I know is I was satisfied. I didn't care if I had made it home and eaten a good meal or if my parents got a call about my behavior or whatever. I don't truly remember what happened after that. Maybe in my subconscious, I remember or maybe it can be recalled, but a lot of things in my past have been recollections of a lot of different things. A lot of things have been foreseen and proven from my visions and acted out by what I call players. Some I intend to believe purposely and others not. Some just fit in as being seen as haters or a hater's helper, but I still consider them players. My father told me once, "We are all players in the game of life." At the time, he was talking about the streets, the dope game, and on how the game was meant to get in and out of. How it has been the same game for years and how some of the people involved in it go in the same paths as the ones before. These weren't his exact words, but it held true to me in different ways to this day. I remember being trustworthy, or at least the feeling of it, and trusting others only to be blindsided, physically hit on the head, and mistreated, but each time, I was enabled by a self-determined strength to not let anyone have the ability to "fuck with me." I was never going to submit or give in to something that would try to belittle me, take advantage, and control me or just do whatever they think they want to do with me like I was just go let. It is never a just go let with me. That is one of the meanings of how I feel that a MF can't fuck with me 'cause they know I'm not just gonna let them. They would have to sneak or manipulate help from others to do close to whatever wrong they wanted to do towards me.

I had been seeing illusions, hallucinations, voices, spirits, ghosts, aliens, or whatever you want to call it from when I was a toddler. They all have been helpful, an annoyance, funny and hateful, inspiring, and draining. I always either appreciated or downplayed them all the while receiving help and information that strengthened my character.

I had been trying to stay out the way of drama, but my choice to do so has me labeled a fuck nigga. It has been me acting like a fuck nigga, wanting to fight and steal and not give a care about the next person, place, or thing. On the other side, I was keeping to myself, trying to improve myself, listening to the elders in my family, and keeping out of the way of being a victim to others and was still labeled a fuck nigga. All the way to being more active on protecting myself and being and doing more for myself, helping others, realizing the more fakeness in others, and not getting violent with them, trying to stay further out the way and still labeled a fuck nigga. I love me! I don't have to and don't want to sell my soul, sell out my relations with the ones who I consider strong in friendships, staying away from the ones I don't consider healthy relations with. I love me! An old acquaintance told me when he was confronted on his behavior and actions of some foul things he had done, "I ain't shit," and left it like that. Like that was it, that was "go solve all the foul and hurt caused." I can't do that fully. I can be proud of being a fuck nigga, but I can communicate the foul things I have done to a point where that person or group of people could understand my situation. I can admit it hasn't always been like that, but it has only been seen not like that by people who already had a fixed foul idea of me. There are a lot of situations that were viewed by those types of people I could influence without trying. A lot of times, I didn't have to say anything or have any explanation of my behavior or actions because I kept to myself and just reacted, instead of provoking others. The others who saw can admit that they would have done the same thing.

In my early years of development, I had crooked teeth, and as a toddler, I would crawl and feel on the lower parts of the legs near the ankles and calf of Black women who came to visit my mother and White women in the grocery stores through their stockings or pantyhose—the feeling of the material and the smoothness was my fun thing. They thought I was so adorable and cute. I think that was when I first learned about sexuality. In fact, at the early ages between three and six, I had my first sexual intercourse. It was with a young neighborhood girl on the next street. When her family would come visit mine, we would play upstairs.

We would play "look at me" in the bed and in the bathroom. I would look inside her vagina. I was amazed by the color and how it looked inside. We eventually stopped playing look-see, and we began to have intercourse. I don't even know who taught me, but it was natural. Still to this day, I remember the smell of young flesh and tend to stay away from it. I never wanted to be accused of doing anything to anyone's child. I never liked being in the car with someone's child by myself and never liked being left alone with someone else's child. I don't let someone's child sit on my lap without the mother's permission, and I will not have a child on my lap if I had a drink or marijuana thing going on around or about me.

I say this because while the girl on the next street and I were playing look-see and started doing other things, I heard that she was being molested by her mother's boyfriend. I always wondered about her sexual mentality later and that still bothers me to this day. Even though I didn't know what I was doing with her after hearing that at that early age, I didn't know if I was a contributor to mentally abusing her or in a helping manner. It did abuse me and help me though. I became desensitized to touches from men. I remember being over their house, which my family and I rarely went over to, and being with her in the closet, and the father slash mother's boyfriend went in there to play with her. I was just standing there, and I felt a funny sensation going through my buttocks. I saw it funny because it was like a mental tinkling of a manure coming out between my butt cheeks. I also say funny because I saw it like looking in the back of my head, and it was like a cartoon or something, like a crayon doodle line. It was very, very quick like I had squirted out some boo-boo out, but I didn't.

The father slash mother's boyfriend only came in the closet for about thirty to forty-five seconds. He said he wanted to play with her and check on us, but he was followed in the room by her mother. He left and said he was going somewhere, to the store or something. I didn't feel my pants go down or anything physically touching me, but I clearly do remember the incident. I didn't complain to anyone because I didn't feel that there was any harm done. I didn't smell anything and I felt fine. I didn't realize that, that may have been my first illusion until later in life, looking at flashbacks of my life when my mind first crashed and I was labeled a schizophrenic.

Another earlier experience of early illusions and hearing voices was times at my family's house where I grew up. At an early age, I would lay in front of the stereo in the dining room and see music. I heard not only the music, but I also saw the artist as family members, and I would receive information as cartoonlike illusions or hallucinations. I would see the artist's faces as cartoons, and they would tell me certain things, certain things that I saw in the future to be true about the music industry and the presentation of music in the future during my older years. It would happen all the time. I could sit there and listen to older family members talking about anything. I was so young that I wasn't interested in what they were saying, and after a few years, the illusions and hallucinations turned into just a voice or voices talking to me. Then in later years, it would simmer down from voices talking to me to certain words that would stick out in the song, and the reference of the voice and voices would be heard.

Words like every I would hear as Eric and I would think that the artist was mentioning me. It was funny to me. It started to fit into what was going on in my life, but I was always listening to music, and it was a big influence in my life. It was the times and current things in life.

I remember songs from Cameo and Black power movement era, songs that I could identify with. Cameo's song "Super Freak" was teaching me about the nature of women, and Candy taught me about the wants of men and women sexually. Growing up, being taught by music and television was not my only way of receiving information. I had an older sister, and I came from a two-parent household. I understood that the man was supposed to have the upper hand in the household and family and relations with a woman. I would also learn from my grandparents and my mother about the world where I came from genealogically and the direction that my family and kinds of people came from and are going. My great-grandmother on my father's side was big on God. She used to ask me all the time, "Do you believe in God?" I used to answer yes. I am not sure if I did or not; I was just saying it to please her honestly. Later on, I started to feel like she was hexing me by making me say, "yes, I believe!" I think I was just tired of her asking every time she came to town.

She used to tell me stories of how the people used to beat her, and she would forgive them and pray to God and for me to do so as well. I didn't like the fact that people had beaten my great-grandmother. She was an older Indian-looking woman. She had silver-like gray hair. She had a deformity on her knee. It was a big clump of bone mass from falling, trying to get on the public transportation while holding my father. She had slipped and started to fall, at the same time she prevented him from getting hurt, and I guess the mass of bone lump was a reminder. I always felt funny when she talked about God. I always wanted to challenge her. I later learned that the people who used to beat her, which I could only understand as them getting over her, were actually fighting and taking advantage of her. I later found out that those same people came back to her later in life and apologized and gave her gifts. I associated with it, and I also think of the apologies and gifts given as an act of God's blessing.

I learned a lot from her, but I still didn't want to believe that you should forgive because that is what God wants you to do and still have problems with forgiving those who have done wrong to me.

C h a p t e r   2

Early Church and Grade School Years

My relationship with God at an early age, I do not know about. My great-grandmother spoke about him, her, it, whoever it is supposed to be from a biblical point of view. I always tried to understand the biblical God, but I always had questions and was challenging, even if I held my questions, thoughts, and ideas to myself.

I remember going to church during my grade school years. It was a Catholic Church, and I was praying and singing in the pews. I had bad experiences early in the pews. My father would always get loud with me in church in front of others and in the public. He wanted me to sing and say the praises loud enough for others in the pews and congregation to see and hear me. I used to cry, and he would still be hard on me about singing and reciting the praises and not mumbling. I hated going to church when he went with us.

Then I started to do more in the church. I became a choir boy and an altar boy. I was baptized, received communion, and I was confirmed. We used to wear the black robes and white top while being an altar boy. I used to always wonder if I would get touched improperly by the priest. I had seen and heard so many things on Tv about Catholic priests. Sometimes he would let us drink the leftover wine in the back. All the priests that were there during my time of being an altar boy were cool. There was no funny business. I appreciated them and learned a lot about religion from them, also the nuns in the Catholic school that was associated with the church. They taught me and the other students how to read the Bible for how it was written at the times. One nun who was special to me taught me how to negate the Bible as well from being as the words of God but the meanings of the miracles and sayings of Jesus and others in the Bible. I am glad that I went to that school. I wouldn't trade that experience to this date, even though my sister and I were only put in the church as members to go to the school for the name of coming from better school education.

I flunked second grade and was said to have been a class clown. One time, my teacher sent home a progress report with me to give to my mother, and I opened it and read it. I folded the bad part of the message, wet it at the fold line, and tried to tear it off and make it look professional. When my mother got it, she asked what happened to it. I lied and told her a big gust of wind came, and it flew into the water on the street of the curb and that I went to pick it up, and it tore, and I tried to fix it. I still get laughed at by my mother to this day about that lie that everyone knew was not true. I straightened up in school and began to do more choir and one time did a talent show performance in the third grade. My older sister went to the school too. I saw her sometimes. I didn't know that she had problems with the teachers there. After the talent showcase, we went home, and my father gave me a hug and told me he was proud of me. He then went to the backyard and started grabbing tree branches off of the tree from the backyard. He had grabbed some big branches. I didn't know what he was doing. I went upstairs to my room, and then I heard it—he was whipping the shit out of my sister with those branches. These were no switches. I started to cry 'cause I didn't want my sister to get hurt or die.

Apparently, my sister had an attitude problem with the nuns and teachers there. She had been cursing at them, being disrespectful. I didn't know anything about it. I was doing good in school and all that, but I still didn't think she deserved the damn backyard trees. I heard her screaming and yelling. All I could do was cry. My mother came in and started hugging me and praising me for doing better in school than the previous years. My dad even made my sister clean all the leaves up. I was like, *Goddamn!* I was scared to see her the next day. I thought she was going to get mad at me. I always loved my sister. My great-grandmother and grandmother on my father's side used to say I always was concerned about her more than me. Every time I would get something from someone, I always asked if she could get some or if they had something for her.

I really didn't care about God too much in my early years. I had no reason to. I guess because I didn't feel that I was doing anything wrong to ask for forgiveness for. Some people turn to God to acknowledge him, her, it, or whatever it is or to give thanks for the many blessings or just to forgive them. I was a decent kid like any other. The aspect of God was brought to me by my elders who had a strong belief system from the South and a need for an advantage in America. The early illusions and hallucinations were closer to being God to me than the teachings and questions that I could only have forced answers for. The illusions and hallucinations were realer and personal back then, more protective and nourishing. Later on in life, I still could see them like that, but I see them as a burden in many way as well. I do not let the influences of others deter me from seeing the true nature of the illusions and hallucinations if my own intake of learning and adjusting to what I was learning had a major part of the change in seeing the helpfulness and concern of the illusions, hallucinations, or spirits as something that needed to be diminished.

All I know is that now I tend to try to get rid of them instead of embracing them. When I was younger, I didn't think of getting rid of them, and there was no struggle in recognizing the nature of what I was adhering. I do not know if my pineal gland has been blocked from all the fluoride and foods and/or if the synchronized information from television and radio frequencies and what was not a part in play over the years. I do and I am glad that I can remember the innocence.

When I was younger, the neighbors down the street and I had plenty of funny issues. At least in my opinion. My one older friend had a grandmother and grandfather who raised him and his siblings. There were two others with him (Keith) being the youngest. His grandfather used to always say I was hardheaded: "That boy hardheaded!" I never knew why but then later found out that there was another saying that "a hard head makes a soft ass." Keith, who was older than me by a couple of years, and the younger neighbor Hank—who I used to always get into li'l fights—with always listened to their grandparents and parents as far as defense for themselves, which would make them seem normal. I always gave them credit for that, but some of the things that they did besides that were kind of corny to me. I always saw Keith who was raised by his grandparents and whose grandmother used to babysit me. She was a kind and gentle li'l old lady until you outgrow the pinches-on-the-cheeks stage like everyone else. Then the older women just became nosier than anything, but you love 'em and deal with 'em, even if it means lying on occasion to avoid things.

Anyway… they would listen to the parents and or grandparents, but behind closed doors, they were mad corny like they couldn't behave themselves. Then Keith would cut my hair and always have his penis pressed on me while doing so and had a funny big gorilla hand in his room. I never understood the gorilla hand, but I did understand the pressing of his penis on me to a point. At first I would think, *Well, he needs to get the job done right*, but then it would go into a thought of *Goddamn!* Then would go into thoughts of when Hank once let his dog hump him in the butt with his clothes on when he bent over from time to time. I used to think I got some weirdo friends for real. I even remember one time going to Hank's house and his brother was pushing my head to the bed. Then my sister walked in, and they were acting like we were playing fighting. I remember another time when Hank and his brothers acted like they were going to hit me over the head in the basement on the love cushion, which was what was called later on during Hank and my high school years. I used to think about the weirdness of the hood friends that I was closer to while getting my hair cut by someone else. I grew out of it, but I do not go to the barber that much anymore. Basically not at all. It is funny how weird things you experience as a child has you doing what seems to be weird now, but I save money not going to the barber, and I save my lack of clowning them as weirdo fag-type motherfuckers. I use that slang or derogatory language because it brings me strength, and I guess I was and will be a fuck nigga when mentioning them from my memories.

My friend Keith who had the big gorilla hand in his room was funny to me in other ways because my father used to bring up the guiding hand in, talking about economics. My father's grandmother—my great-grandmother—would always say that people don't use their hands anymore. She also used to say that life was like a hand, from small thumb to small pinkie. You are born a baby, needing someone to take care of you; you go through life growing and getting stronger and then gradually shrink back down to small fingers or baby-like conditions that you need to be taken care of. I mixed the power of the hand from the guide of economics to the gorilla hand because we were cool friends. I looked up to him on a lot of things and felt good about him and his accomplishments. We used to look at porn magazines in my parents' basement and almost had a sex trade turn on a couple neighborhood females in my parents' basement, one of the girls being my sister. He was with the neighbor girl three houses down and was with my sister. I had already been sexually somewhat experienced and knew what to do. I didn't know anything about taboo or nothing, but I did know right from wrong. I didn't have sex with my sister as the situation suggested. I saw my sister go upstairs and turn to me, saying nothing, but I knew that she was also glad that it did not happen. He got some, but I didn't with the neighbor girl. I did get to see the neighbor girl's hairy vagina, and I wanted to have sex with her too. She was older and athletic, and I was a li'l chubsy-ubsy. I just liked seeing the hair on the girl's vagina.

Once Keith got to high school, it seemed as though he tried to use his power of hand to herb me or treat me like I was a just a youngster. Once he asked me to pull my penis out, and I refused. And when I became a freshmen at the same high school he was already attending, on the first day, he wanted me to hold his belt while walking in. I refused then too. Once we got to high school, I saw all the previous gay and weird things about my neighborhood close friends differently. I was prouder that we were all doing and trying to do well. It is funny how I still remember those small things, but are they actually small things or the beginning of a paranoid mind state? We all had high sexual energies at that point in our lives.

One time, he came by, and we were talking in the basement, and he noticed the dirty laundry in the laundry room. He grabbed some of my sister's panties and noticed a stain on them in the crotch area. He was happy to say that my sister was on her period. He was so hyped about it. I was afraid he was going to tell everyone, and I was going to get in trouble for even letting him grab the damn thing. She was my sister; I didn't let anything foul happen to her, and even though words, they say, can't hurt you, it would still be me bringing negative energy to her.

Every time I think about energy, I think about God. When those commercials used to say God is moving supernaturally, I always froze like I hoped it didn't get me. That was when I was younger. I used to think I saw something moving either from behind the reverend, or fake reverend I thought at the time, on the TV infomercial. I either saw something moving from behind him or from in front, wherever I saw the propaganda rushing or racing to grab and tell the world. I used to see a bunch of illusions or propaganda, especially at an early age of I think about five or six to thirteen years of age.

At an age when I was starting to go visit more than sit at home or just playing outside, I had a setback of two hip surgeries. One broke from jumping ramps on my bike. I remember it hurting afterward one time when I landed funny on the bike seat after jumping a ramp. We used to get bricks or big rocks and place them under wood planks and ride our bikes over them really fast like we were Evel Knievel. When I went to the doctor, they told me my hip had slipped out of place. I had surgery and missed on going to school. But from sitting at home and watching TV and my father bringing me Wendy's and all types of fast food, like Mr. Hero and McDonald's I gained weight, and the pressure from being big, gaining weight, and putting all that pressure on one leg from the crutches made the other hip slip after the first one healed. So I had two surgeries on my hips, actually four. One to put in the pins in the hips for placement and the other to take out the pins. Two sets of surgeries on each hip. I missed school, I think, for the entire year, but I had home tutors, and my school assignments and homework were delivered to me.

I was bad when I was in my early years before the incident with my sister and the tree limbs in the backyard and my father whipping her and making cry for her. I mooned the older White people in the donut shop down the street and got in big trouble with the nuns at my school. They were disgusted that I would represent their school and pulled my pants down and show my fat Black butt to people. This was back when you were the school's responsibility until you made it inside your home and were with an older youth or an adult.

My sister and I were latchkey kids, but I just slipped that day being too silly, probably from the sugary donuts. Donuts and other food tasted better back then. We used to get food all the time after school. The school had certain lunch days for pizza and hot dogs. Those were even better back then. Those hot dog and buns were warm in the buns and had a distinct taste. It is funny how I can still remember the freshness of the food back then. We used to go to a pizza place, a sub place, and a hamburger place after school. They were all great. Then my sister and I started cooking at home for ourselves.

One time, I almost caught the house on fire from a grease fire that I didn't know how to control. My stupid li'l self didn't know *not* to add water to a grease fire. We didn't get the kitchen repainted and fixed till years later. It wasn't too much damage, just some color damage on the walls. But when I was eating fast food or food already prepared like when I was in early grade school or when I was home-schooled…*woooww*. Those were the days. I ate and watched TV all day. I watched *Gilligan's Island*, *I Love Lucy*, *Bonanza*, and then I had access to cartoons before everyone else. I was watching stuff like *Gobots*, *Thunder Cats*, *He-Man*, *Robotech*, and all the other super action figure cartoons before they came on again, when everyone else was out of school. I think that might be the time I started to have more hallucinations and illusions more frequently. I started to see propaganda for what it really was.

I couldn't play sports, and before the hip surgery, I always had trouble making the teams. I was always chubby as a child. My older female cousin said that I would lose the weight once I got more interested in girls, but I was already interested in girls. Anyways… I had a problem with my chest when I was younger. I had titties from being fat. One time, at a basketball tryout, I wore a brown elastic knee wraparound my chest so my titties wouldn't be flopping running up and down the court. I saw others with underdeveloped chests, but they were slimmer and taller. I knew I had to start working out. My father bought a weight-lifting bench set a few years after that. I wanted to work out not only to develop muscles but to get rid of the man talking in my head from watching too much TV.

I used to see and hear illusions, hallucinations, spirits, ghost, or whatnots from a very early age. I remember my grandmother saying after a long trip from coming down South back to my parents' place up north, "If me and this family have done anything wrong to you, God will strike my house down by a tornado." Something kept telling me to accept her words, but I kept telling it no, I didn't want it to happen. It kept begging me and trying to plea with me to accept her words and let it happen. I kept telling it I didn't want to. I never had trouble down south with my grandparents on my father's side nor my great-grandmother, who I adored. I did have a couple of incidents down there but nothing serious. Once my grandmother smacked me in the face for not going to bed and having my mouth open when she would try to discipline, me but then she grabbed my sister and I, took us for ice cream in our PJs in the middle of the night, but that was some years ago before this trip. On one trip, an incident happened. My sister and I got into a big fight, and she grabbed a knife. I opened my shirt and held my hands and arms spread wide open, like, "Do it! Go ahead and do it." My two older boy cousins were there holding me back, but they really thought it was funny. I never had a reason to want to do any harm to my family. Even though things were getting sour with my sister, I still just thought it was just our relationship 'cause for a point in time, we always physically fought. I didn't want my granny's house to suffer because of some nonsense.

Another time I heard voices was when I was young, without being diagnosed when I was at the end of junior high school. I was asleep in the basement on the couch and woke up to a voice, saying,

"Move over." It was a female's voice but no one was there. It wasn't one of those things where I was caught between sleep and being awake… I had just woken up, but it had been more than five to seven minutes already. I never told anyone about her. She later might have saved my life or might have been the thing harassing me, or both. I do know that TV is something else that is constantly on the mind.

I had always watched TV since before the acceptance of the gay balloons or gay pride movement parades that has been highly acclaimed now. I remember shows that were supposed to be positive cartoons but were making being bad funny. I remember it stemming from chasing Road Runner to me chasing, or at least coming outside, with a knife because I was tired of being bullied or seen as weak by the older and not-too-much-older homies in the hood. I remember the "Frickle Frackle" of the cartoons and what they meant as bad language to my father having to wash my mouth out with soap and in front of the neighborhood friends to see. I remember them laughing and looking at me funny, even looking with those "I told you so" eyes.

Then after that time of being back home for schooling 'cause of the surgeries, the TV used to talk to me. While being at home during those times and after to now, I always heard voices from the TV. I later in life called it the TV Man. It is not and hasn't always been a man's voice, but distinctively, the male voice is a clear representation of the government or authority. I started not only hearing voices from the TV but could see the person such as newscasters and others actually saying what I was hearing from their mouths, like that was just what it was.

It grew into an impression in my mind that the people of this country knew me and knew what kind of person I was. I even experienced personal deep-down secrets being exposed by the TV Man.

One time, my father walked past in the hallway between the upstairs bedrooms, and I had a questioning look on my face, and I asked in my head, "What is it?" hoping to ask him in a special way.

I saw and heard in return from him, "It is the devil!" The illusion that I saw was a gold thin-like figure inside my father's body that answered.

I knew the answer didn't come from his mouth but from something else. I later learned to respect the aspect of seeing a gold tone on people of color, even the darkest-skinned person, I could see shimmer of gold within the texture of their skin. I saw things brought forth by my own mind from the illusions of the TV Man or propaganda of the situation in the city of Chicago and the folks and people of the nation and taxation of workers for the gangs. I saw a message from Stanley "Tookie" Williams to not give up and keep being gangster with what I intended to do in life. It was a message taken from me by an illusion of a man riding to different cities and shooting and killing people. He wouldn't stop, and his reasoning was for the better advancement and for others to understand the struggle of his people. He was respected by niggas, and even the press had dubbed him as a troublesome hero that they just let do because they couldn't stop him. I saw the cartoonish illusions of a gangster Crip riding up, popping the shit out of motherfuckers every time an injustice was done or was in the news by White people. I took the message as to not quit or give up fighting for what I believed was right. I saw illusions I believe that later came true, such as who and at what time during the country's history would be president. I saw most of the mass shootings and bombings before they happened, damn near twenty years before they happened.

It was to the point where I was watching reruns on TV at a later stage in my life. Eventually, the government's voice turned into more voices like the newscasters and anyone who it had wanted to be. Sports games and any other events were fun to watch, but sometimes a deep personal quote or exposing line about my life experiences or personality would get under my skin that I would have heard from the TV, and I would get pissed and turn it off. It is funny how the mind works and the eyes associate with the other senses and the function attached make a reality as far as you let it take you. It was like my mind and eyes were giving me so much information that maybe I functionally couldn't keep up, and I had to focus on seeing other things in illusion and hallucination type of ways, or maybe that is how God wanted me to see and be knowledgeable of things.

Junior High School and Early High School Years

My junior high school at the same grade school was not that interesting. A couple of sex offers, a hoped to be girlfriend, and many accounts of listening to other's sexual experiences. I had already had sex when I was way younger, but in my junior high years, I was just masturbating like every other young man during that experimental age. I did see a lot of things from girls showing there vagina hairs in the gym to guys getting beaten up by guys from other schools because they didn't want to have sex with a certain girl.

I do remember one girl who I was very fond of. I don't know what happened to me, but one day, I was just staring at her, and my tongue started licking my lips extremely slow while looking at her. She caught eye contact and started doing it back. I was shocked because I didn't know that I was doing it. I guess that was the first time that my mind used my body for motion by itself. I had later asked her for her number scared out of my mind thinking she would laugh at me. She gave it to me, and we talked for an evening but got cut short on the phone by me getting hanged up on. I later learned when her friend called, that she was sorry for the hang-up, and had to get off the phone because of her parents. We never hooked up or talked about sex or being boyfriend and girlfriend again ever. It was like the situation was just flat-out over.

I once again tried for the basketball team in the school that was involved with the CYO League. I didn't make it, even though my handles had improved from grade school. I still couldn't jump high, and my layups were usually blocked. It was offered to be the ball boy and then the scorekeeper. I did that job for like one or two games but got tired of how it had looked for me. No one wants to be a water boy.

This was also the time that I became more interested in making music. We in the neighborhood had always been big on music and the ways of the times. I remember Wham! and Menudo, but I also remember the Art of Noise group and the many instrumentals and breakbeat remixes. We used to get boxes of appliances that came in that were on people's lawn for the trash and broke them down, spread them into a large piece, and would breakdance on them. This was the same time as the movies glorified break dancing. Movies like *Breakin'* *1* and *2* and *Beat Street* were the best. We started to rap early and started making tapes against each other in the hood. The other side or the group that my two friends—Hank and Tom—and I were in were against the other streets in the hood that had a snitch and everything. One time, he heard us practicing a recording in Hank's family basement who lived down the street. Sylvester was listening through the window and yelled, "One, four, six, I'm the snitch!" Sylvester was from 146th Street. He was with another homie who lived on 144th, who was big on music. He was rapping and deejaying. After they heard us practicing, they went out with a song called "ESP." I guess they felt they had eyes and ears everywhere.

Our technique for making music was stuffing wet paper or putting tape over the nipped-out top end of prerecorded factory tapes. We would use a boom box or house stereo unit and record and pause the intros to songs that had no words on them. We would do this over and over again. Soon, we would have two to three minutes of looped music. Then the tape we recorded the looped music onto would be our beat tape, and we would record either with the small microphones that came with the boom boxes and home units, or we would just rap right into the headphones that were plugged into the microphone jack. The hood always had bragging rights as the first to do hood battle rap. It wasn't violence or anything. We were just having fun, and it was much fun. We had and still have a lot of pride in those works.

During this time as well was when the hood started to sell crack. My friends weren't major with it at first. I remember hearing about having to re-up and how much and what prices were, but I never knew who they were getting it from. My father made me swear to never sell drugs. The way he said it at first was "Boy, if you be out there selling that shit, I'mma kill you!" Then he calmed down and asked me to swear to never sell drugs. I later broke that promise when I purchased a quarter pound of weed to sell as an adult. When I mean later in life, I mean *way* later after my father retired and got property to rent. I was in one of his properties, living as a tenant, and it seemed as though the weed was coming up missing, but it was really due to the fact that my homeboy who had been in the dope game for years was arrested and known. He had sold me a garbage sack to sell. All the weed I used to buy from him for personal use was great. The sacks were green and smelled and blew good smoke to get high off of. The one sack I bought to sell from him was garbage. It was filled with seeds and big, long sticks and was black. I felt like it was a challenge…like if I could get this off, I was deemed a true drug hustler. I had packaged it right, separating the seeds from the weed and tearing the long sticks and stems off before putting it in the baggies. I had to sell them as bigger weight for a lower price just to make it pleasing to buy. The weed was straight boo-boo, and even though I packaged it correctly for presentation, you could still tell by looking at it that is was boo-boo. Well, I got it off with no profit gained and no profit loss. I just made my money back. I hope my promise that I made during my late junior high school years still stands. I felt then that the dope game wasn't for me. I felt that if my own homeboy would sell me some garbage to sell, knowing money is important, then I should either find another connection or quit while I was ahead and didn't take a full loss in the dope hustle game.

I had some great friends in junior high that stemmed from grade school. I had plenty of experiences with teachers, my grades, and getting held back a grade because of my behavior to getting picked on and beaten up by bullies in my own grade to upper grades. Once I had a triple fat goose winter coat on, and the hood was zipped up. A classmate and one of his older buddies had beaten me up, but I didn't feel it through the zipped-up hood. I knew I was getting hit and was crying, but I really didn't feel the blows and punches to my head. That was usually how it was for me in my dealings with life, period.

As I would study myself later and continued to gain knowledge of self, I learned that people who have been negative or violent or have had some type of animosity toward me really never knew me but was frustrated or misunderstood my light and nature. Usually, once we had an altercation or conversation, we were good. It was just the guys that beat me up that morning at recess, nothing major.

My one homeboy Hank from the hood who lived down the street later was in my school and classes. This is the same homeboy who we used to record music in his basement with, and I used to go over when I was younger than these years. This is the same homeboy who I was going to sneakily apologize to. The same homeboy who beat me up and used to block my shots in the older homey backyard, playing basketball. He now in, our later years of junior high school, became a closer friend. During graduation, we decided to walk a certain walk different from everyone else. The nuns got mad as we walked during graduation. They wanted us to hurry up, and we both had smirks on our faces. I had plenty of cool friends in junior high—White, Black, Oriental, and Latin or maybe he was Hispanic—but my hood homeboy was one of the ones who came from another school to do junior high school years in.

I remember his mother asking me how to get him involved in going to a Catholic school, and she told me of the benefits that she thought they would give him. His mother was cool, and I liked talking to her. I told her to call my mom. I really didn't know how to specifically get in the school. I didn't know if he would have to go through the same processes I did going in as a first grader.

During the end of our junior high school years, we had to choose what high school to go to. I chose the same one as one as the older homey Keith from the neighborhood went to. The same homie who used to cut my hair. Even though at times I thought he was weird, I still looked up to him because he was doing things that I wasn't since he was older and had opportunities, and my parents felt safe with me going there and him being there. My hood homey Hank, who I walked funny style with during graduation, decided to go there too. I remember after graduation that summer seeing him on the block, just taking in the atmosphere of the hustle and bustle of *G*s and dope dealers. He said he was getting ready for if anything had jumped off at the new schoolhouse.

I thought he was crazy 'cause I knew that if something was to happen, it would be so quick that the hood wasn't going to be there or arrive in time. The hood had ways of looking out for us when we were in high school. The hood was comprised of two high schools. The block was split between two cities. The main city and a suburb that was all Black so it was deemed a ghetto. It wasn't all Black when I was younger. I remember older White folks and even one young White couple and their kids in a house on my street. About a year later, the old White man with the runny nose, who used to just let it hang from his nose, died. Then it was basically all Black people there.

Going to an all-boys high school was great. It was one of the best decisions I had ever made. The only thing I learned was geometry and algebra. Everything else I had already learned in grade and junior high school. I used to fall asleep in religion studies classes. The nuns at my previous school made sure we knew how to read the Bible in two ways—one in full faith and the other logically. With it being all boys, it was different from my grade school because the guys would say just about anything and fights would break out so frequently. The fights would break out, and then that was it. No one really ever got in trouble for fighting. I guess it was a guy thing.

We used to get initiated as freshmen. That year was funny. You never knew what upperclassman would come behind you and strong-arm you for your books or drill you in the chest at your locker. It was more of a love thing than an abusive one. At least that was how I took it. One time, one classmate slapped the shit out of me in class right in front of the teacher. I swore I was going to get back at him after classes, outside at the bus stop. Well, I went to the bus stop late…I had just missed the bus. I saw it pull off. We caught the city bus line to and from school. He was at the bus stop, sitting like he was waiting for me. It was just me and him. He said he didn't want it. I don't know what changed his mind. I didn't think it was my little reputation of judo classes that I took when I was younger. Maybe the hood had stepped in. Maybe my older homey from the hood who attended there had said something, I don't know. We both sat there and became cool. It was fights almost every other day; school was fun.

I went out for the football team knowing that I had a heart murmur condition from when I was a toddler. I just wanted to try. Ha! I couldn't run a damn lap. Practice would have been cool if it wasn't for the conditioning. All the exercises were the ones I didn't want. I couldn't keep running laps. I was always chubby, and it showed. I received a lot of sympathy and support from the older players on the bus going home from practice. I didn't think that they were clowning, but I never knew what was said when I got off the bus. I felt then that if I couldn't play, and I damn sure wasn't going to take a water boy or stats keeper position like I did for the CYO League in grade school and junior high. I knew I might as well make some money.

So I got a job with a local grocery store. It wasn't my first job. My first job was working at my grandmother's alteration shop. I used to clean and take the trash out for her. She paid me, and it brought the value of work into my life. At this job, I started off as a grocery bagger, and I had to get a work permit because I was only fifteen years old. I stayed at that job for all four years of high school until I left for college. I met plenty of people and all types of people at that job. The employees, the managers, the customers were all a pleasant experience. I did have one experience that almost got me fired, though.

On a weekend, before I left for work, my mom asked me to bring home some dishwasher powder. I didn't have any money, and I knew it, but my dumbass didn't ask for any before I left. I was planning to steal some real slick like. See, we—the fellow baggers and I— had been getting over the system by clocking each other in and out for extra hours. The managers didn't know because they were always asking us to stay and calling us in for extra hours.

Everyone was stealing, either putting things in the manager's office like they bought it during break or putting it in the break room and taking it out later. I had grabbed the dishwashing powder, and at the end of the night, I grabbed it to leave only to be called back by the Black assistant manager. He made a big deal of it. He wanted a receipt and even looked through the register tape in full if the cashier I said had rung me out. He couldn't find the transaction. I thought I was done for. I swore up and down that I had paid for it when I had bought it on my break.

He even got mad at the cashier—a Black lady who probably needed the job more than I did because she had kids. I was so scared but stood to my beloved truth that I had purchased it. The cashier looked at me in disgust, but I didn't feel her until I started making my way home… I was like, *Wheeewww*. I told my mom about that, and she was upset but glad that I didn't get fired. I think that was when I started to feel that stealing was okay. I stole from my mother before.

Once a high school friend of mine named Gevis, and now great friend, used to go hit the streets and look for prostitutes. We got turned out by his older cousin, who also went to the same high school. He was a couple of years grade ahead of us. Gevis used to drive his mother's car. We used to hit different strips in the city. I had the time of my life looking for whores. I used to get mad when we couldn't see or find any to mess with. Gevis used to laugh and bring up jokes like, "Hey, hoes have to go in and eat and use the bathroom too!" I guess I was only seeing them as objects and not as real people; I later earned a work certification in sex and drug counsel work and did part-time, not as an abusive gorilla pimp but as a chauffeur, scheduler, and security style of pimping.

My main thinking from high school was that I was a part of the he-man woman haters club that stemmed from watching *The Little Rascals*. I used to get girls from both sides of the track—the workers on the corner and the good girls in school. Later on in my life with the way of the world, it was hard to tell the difference between the two types except for the extremely strung-out-on-dope girls. Yep, I went in my mother's purse and stole her ATM card and took eighty out of her account for me and Gevis to go tricking on some street whores. I had used my mother's card before with her permission. She had trusted me and would always tell me to grab her purse when she was about to give me some money. She often used to tell me just to get it out, depending if she was lying down or not. Well, once again, I got caught. My mother noticed the money missing from her account a couple of days later. We were sitting at the dining room table as usual. She told me that the bank was doing an investigation on her account. She further told me she had some money missing. I quickly told her what I did. I didn't tell her what it was for. I told her I was with my friend, and we wanted to get something to eat. Since she was sleep, I didn't want to wake her. My lying ass avoided the embarrassment of admitting I was addicted to tricking, but I lost her trust anyways. I was shaking like a motherfucker at the table when I was telling her. I wasn't scared of going to jail or anything like that. It was just the fact of admittance and shame. I had to admit it because she was mentioning cameras at the ATMs and how thorough they were talking of investigating. Then when I told her that I was with my friend, she was still protective of me. She was saying and asking if he had me do it or if he had done it. I assured her no, that he didn't. I really didn't want him to get in any trouble and didn't want the situation to spread further than the table. I apologized over and over and swore to pay it back and lied again and said that that was the original plan anyways and that I just forgot to tell her. I knew I lost her trust for a while, but once again, she gave me trust with handing her purse to her.

I was bad in high school, even though I had a job and average grades. I don't know if it was the job that had and me not caring about things, if it was the ways of the time and the ease of being able to turn to the streets and neglecting my promise to my father, or if it was just an evil nature in me. All I know is during that time, I didn't have any voices from the TV Man or any irregular illusions or information about anything in a mental health issue type of way except once, and it later changed my life. A life lesson that I still stick to is never talk shit with no intention of action and never underestimate anyone or any situation.

In class once in sophomore year, I got into an argument with a White boy. I don't remember what the argument was about, but the teacher who was also the head football coach sent me to the hallway. I swore I was going to kick the White boy's ass. I waited outside the hallway making gestures, holding my fist to my jaw, trying to scare him through the open doorway. I waited so long outside in the hallway that I unpumped myself. When class was over, I went to the door while everyone was leaving, and I was standing there, waiting to see him. I saw him starting to come, and then I saw his friend walk between us. I looked toward his friend as he was walking through, and then *bam!* The motherfuckin' White boy stole on me. I stumbled back and tripped over my own foot and fell. I remember yelling to my high school friends to hit that motherfucka. I saw two to three of them hitting him. Then the teacher came out and dispersed everyone. I got up, and he asked me if I was okay. I said, "Yeah, I'm good!" then went about my day. Everyone expected a fight after school. I tried to meet him by the weight room, which was a place that I enjoyed lifting weights with the either the football or basketball team from time to time. He was in the hallway. One of the football players on the JV and varsity squad, the full back, told me to wait and to not go over there. I didn't. Shortly before the fight, like one to two months previous, three of my friends and I had started a group called the Four Horsemen, named after the wrestlers on TV. We would go around and start fights with the White boys in the hallways, just running up to them and punch drilling them on the lockers. It was fun thing for both sides in my opinion. We used to fuck them White boys up, but it was just a school thing. I worked with some at my job, and it never went over outside of school. I think things would have overextended if I had went over there and started more trouble. I think everyone else had known it too. That was when I knew it was time to start thinking more reasonably about my actions. I would continue to do some outlandish and evil things though.

When I got home, I tried to sleep, and the fight kept coming to me over and over inside my head. It was like something was trying to tell me something. I kept seeing pictures and motion-like illusions of the incident from the outside. I was fully awake, and I was tired of seeing it. I saw different things from what I remember. Then the illusions went into all types of scenarios and events that I definitely never experienced or at least I think I didn't. They were all flashing by and quick. My eyes were so tired. I turned my head on the bed, and it seemed that I was looking down the street in my friend Hank's basement, where we used to make music at. I saw that Black people wanted me to gain my soul back and that I had gotten knocked out by a White boy. Then I had seen that someone had put a finger in my buttocks when I was lying on the ground after I fell from being stole on. Then I saw myself in a dress and being passed around as an example that I had lost my manhood. I saw illusions of me traveling to different cities, looking for my manhood. Then as I kept focusing in on the illusion-type stories, I saw me being raped by my hood homeboys after a recording session and again at a time when I was younger by the community people as a whole for asking one of the younger kids to pull his penis out to pee. I never remembered that. I was hit on the back of the head and information was yelled in my ear, and I was supposed to have astroplane different places. I had even given up my soul to certain groups to be their ghost or protector or energy spirit. I was surrounded by all types of people that were surrounding me in the basement as my homeboys took turns, either molesting me or acting like they were to gain submission to, and in my subconscious, they were yelling things in my ear. One of the homeboys who was originally from the Cleveland side of the hood and went to the Cleveland High School that area was assigned to was reading a Masonic book over me. It was all so fast, but I read and saw every illusion or motion picture clearly and usually saw illusions and things in cartoon.

Then I heard voices of Black leaders telling me that every Black man has a tail. I saw more illusions of me going over to the neighbor's house next door and apologizing for pulling my penis out in front of their kids and going to the sidewalk in front of their house, having a tail of a penis sticking out with the head of the penis sticking out toward the air like I was fucking the pass. I was a black figure, like a devil or something. I remember the incident of pulling my penis out in front of the neighbors' kids, but it was an innocent incident, and an elder neighbor had yelled at me to stop. I was just using the bathroom. One of the kids said he had to pee, and I told him to go ahead and don't be afraid to do so and showed him how to pee properly outside. It was no gay or child molestation type of stuff involved. I was a child myself, but I guess things like that can go on. I remember being asked about the event by a couple of people, and my answers didn't seem to fit the so-called crime, but I mentioned a couple of concerns I had of the behavior of some of the older friends in the hood.

When I got nervous, sometimes I spoke and other times it was like my mouth couldn't move to answer. Seeing those illusions had me wondering later in life. I wondered if they happened like I was seeing them at that point in time of the first illusions. Maybe something was waking me up to see something that happened because I may have been considered a hazard to the community, and in some way, I was forced to forget and never knew it. Later on in life, I heard of cutting off your kids, manipulation techniques, and mind control. It seemed like the entire neighborhood and my own sister was there from time to time while I was going through a certain type of mind manipulation. Seeing and focusing in more on the motion pictures or illusions, I saw that when I was traveling to different places, my family was with me during the astroplane events. I heard gangsters from Arkansas having a gang meeting and noticing that I was there and questioning who I was. The recollection was wild, but I guess that that was all my subconscious would let me see of and if the torturous events took place. I can somewhat understand that the community didn't want things to come out of my mouth, saying things about others in the community that would hamper them and the youth there from future success. That was the way I saw it. I can't say if they were wrong or not because I actually do not remember experiencing the event except from my own bed and the illusions, I guess after the fact. I do remember after turning my head from the illusions in the basement down the street and returning my mind to more concentration to my own bed, my father was walking past, or at least I thought it was him, saying, "You ready? Let's get!" And something rushed out of me and went down the steps with him.

Things continued to be more of an illusion and hallucination from then on out. I saw my DNA being taken from my body; I saw all types of information and information on places and people and all types of scenarios. Later in life, I saw how deep the mind was during travels that I encountered.

I stayed in the room for the next couple of days. I didn't have to work that weekend, and the so-called fight happened on a Friday. I stayed in a stupor of illusions it seemed like they were lessons of either my personal or family history, history of Black people, and nature of people and organizations. I saw the story of DNA being extracted and analyzed from a 1950's point of view. The illusion was black and white and was like a TV documentary. There were stories of me or my information being spread supernaturally like in the religious commercials throughout the White communities as me aware of it and in the Black communities in two ways—the first original way was as someone to be cherished and protected and the other as to be given up and not cared for but not fully disrespected. All the stories were visions of before I was born. Mostly in black and white. I also saw that I might have been a descendant of a slave who had been castrated. I later seemed to experience some of the visions in certain types of ways, none of them full and as brutal as originally seen during the stupor but in more logical and mild ways but still detrimental to a person's life and definitely in the reconstruction of strength in the Black race and community. I saw a visions that I had asked everyone in the world to know me…which I know I never did. I really always tried to stay low-key, especially when I started smoking marijuana heavily in my later years in college.

The girls during high school were always there. Even though I felt that I didn't have to get any girl, there was still pressure to be seen or known to have at least one girl who you could say that you were honestly messing with. I had been tricking with prostitutes and didn't mind doing so, but I wasn't comfortable saying so or having others find out. Girls knew I had some kind of money even though it wasn't dope boy type of money. Girls used to come by the grocery store and look at me and my friends working, but my friends would always get them first. I met a girl that I had started to connect with sexually from my job. She was a cashier, and I used to always try and catch her register to pack the bags for her orders going through. One time, I just kept looking at her ass. She had a nice juicy, round ass and a cute face. I just kept staring, and my body began to do a motion like I was stroking the air. It was uncontrollable. I quickly stopped 'cause I was at work and didn't want to embarrass myself. I didn't know how strong I was doing it until after the fact and felt more embarrassed. I don't know what came over me. She was the first girl I had sex with that I didn't pay for during my high school years. She had a boyfriend, and I was okay with her and her family. Her mother seemed to take a strong liking to me. I was fine being the side thing, but I did want more. I felt everything about her. She would come by my parents' house, and every time we would have sex or try to or would be kissing or something. I liked her brown skin and round, fat ass. She was a perfect size in height and weight for me too. People said we looked good together. I liked her so much I used to pick her from work on days when I didn't even work. I was invested in seeing that she was okay.

One time, her family house didn't have water, and I let her come by and take a shower. My mother was pissed, but she couldn't really do anything because this was someone I was invested with. I mean, she could have it out with the both of us because it was her house, but she knew how I felt about her. I remember one time after giving her oral, the next day, I still had hairs in my teeth. I really only told one person what I did and that was my friend Tony from school, who also worked at the job. I never was the type to brag and boast about having sex with a girl to others. She was the only girl who made me cry during that time. During that time in my life, the homies and I were always screaming, "Fuck that bitch!" She made me cry because we were chillin' in my car in my parents' driveway, and she took my class ring off my finger and wouldn't give it back. It seemed as though she was testing me to hit her or beat her like her boyfriend was doing to her. I cried because I didn't want to hit her and was so frustrated by how she was trying to play that situation like that. It was a mad cry, like "This bitch is crazy! This bitch is really going to go there after all the good nigga boyfriend side good man things I had been and was doing for her." She was in love with her boyfriend I guess; I don't know for sure. She never compared us, but she did bring up sexual differences from time to time. I am glad that I didn't go there that night and hit her. I had never hit a female before, except for my sister, but I didn't consider her a female. Though she is my sister. I love her, but we fought all the time, and I use to nickname her Ugmo, but it was out of affection though. This girl had me crying like a bitch. I wasn't wheezing or nothing like that, but I did want to call my mom to the door and have her give it back to me.

When I think back on it, I can say once again that I am glad that I didn't forcefully put my hands on her. She gave me the ring back, and we never spoke of the situation again. I don't know if she was testing me or felt pity on me for crying. I just knew that I didn't want to be considered in the same classification as her main dude. I am glad that the police didn't have to be called, and I didn't have to go to juvy or had any extra mess that could have occurred from the situation. The crying like a goddamn bitch and how she was acting, testing me, just brought me so much pain like I was being punished for being a good dude, and the stress was too much. After that, I still never hit a female, except for spats with my sister, but I never let up on watching females and the games that could be played by them. So I guess I owe her a recognition for helping create a monster to the female gender later on. I never hit a female or mate, but I always watched them out of the side of my eyes, and I did later on end up robbing a couple females who tried to steal from me. I mean, robbing them and kicking them out of the car at gunpoint and hitting them in areas of the head and face in order to not leave a bruise but leave a lasting impression on them, like hitting a bad dog on the nose with a newspaper.

There was another girl who I was cool with during my senior year of high school, when the school merged with the sister school down the street and went coed. She used to go to my locker and give me a hug all the time and small gifts every once in a while. She once gave me a stuffed cloth penis. I thought she was special. All the Black girls used to look at me funny for a while, but then they stopped when more information got around about the girl from my job and me. I started hearing rumors about my so-called White girlfriend from the hallways and didn't want to hear them. I didn't care if she was White or not. I was pleased that she cared enough to even try to like me and give me gifts. I never had a chance to have sex with her, but that was okay. I had never had sex with a White girl, not even a prostitute, until later years in college. My mother taught me once that love and respect break color lines. She said, "If a White man is willing to love me and respect me and a Black man is willing to just have sex with me, try and control and beat me, I am going to be with that White man!" I always heard that White girls are fun, and later I found that they sure are. I was always a reactive person to racism. I never really had a problem with talking with White females or males because of the schools that I went to; even with the sexual experiences that I encountered later on with White women, I was never uncomfortable and had a great time.

I was starting to get militant during high school, but really, the message of Black empowerment was just being seen and heard more. I had already known the aspects of the Black community and the White world. I had already understood and been through the effects of propaganda and government understanding. It was hip-hop during that time that had me more conscious. I started to hear the names and history of Black leaders and events against and for Black people more and more. The ways I heard them made me want to get more active and act accordingly. We were already getting in physical altercations with the White boys at school heavily just about every spring season. Those weren't the only fights that occurred.

My one homeboy from the same city, but he was the other side of the city, got in a fight with an upperclassman. My friend Ben and I were in our sophomore year when he put the hands on the upperclassman. He did a knee kick right to his face. We all used to play fight with each other, walking down the hallways, but who really had hands when the adrenaline started to rush and the butterflies took effect or when you get hit and felt funny about it enough to quit or feel lightheaded to want to quit? Another time, another friend from the actual city of the greater city, not a suburb, was in a fight with an upperclassman at a fast-food restaurant down the street from the school. They both decided to meet up there to fight. This was freshman year, and we were seen in a different manner than just some lowly freshmen. My friend Gerald put a whooping on ole boy. He was tagging him and then slammed him. Then he was on top and beating him like a gorilla. Gerald got wild at it from rage. He was a beast at that moment in time for sure. He was hitting him in his face with both hands at the same time, pounding him like an animal gone mad. That was when I knew I needed to step up my hands and attack game to defend and attack. These boys weren't playing. I knew they might try to get some rep back and that I might have been a target in the future since I was there, supporting my friend. I was always the bully type and playful, wanting to box and things. One older hood homey and I used to spar up and down the street. He used to box for the police athletic league/ pal 5. He used to tag me, but I was learning his moves. He used to say, "This is my world!" when he used to tear me up. I learned a lot of blocking techniques. We all used to talk about boxing and fighting techniques. Even with my high school friends, we would discuss that on a regular basis.

I never really got in any other one-on-one incidents except the incident with the White boy. We did a lot grouped-up fighting. We had to protect ourselves from another local high school, really all of them. We were considered a big rival because the school was known to excel in sports, and we were deemed as privileged. The one school I just mentioned was a public school. It was attached to my neighborhood. It was the school assigned to the city zone across the street, on the block where the all Blacks were and the suburb that I lived. I lived a block away from the block, so some that went to that school did know me and some were new and older homies.

One time, that school went to my high school for a basketball game, and they caused havoc. I mean total chaos. They were hitting, threatening, and disrespecting anyone they could as long as they weren't from their school. I was never touched by anyone of them. In fact, I saw one of the newer homeboys to the neighborhood just looking at me and smiling while it was going in on, he was hitting other classmates from my school. I was surrounded by all this fighting, just standing there. I didn't know what to do. It was a choice to help friends from my current school and previous school friends who came to my current school as underclassmen or to bang with the hood. Some of them had been underclassmen because I passed my sophomore year at that. The havoc didn't last too long. When it was over, I was glad I was not judged by my schoolmates; at least I don't think so. It was never brought up to me, but it was discussed between my friend Hank, who lived down the street and went to the same school.

Mid-High School to Graduation Years

During basketball season, we used to get into fights from time to time. If it wasn't physical fights, it was a bunch of hoorah and cheering of slander, vulgar language, and disrespect for the other school. At that time, the energy was like magic in the air. The energy was strong and great, and both sides were always full of spirit and strength. Usually, it would be a fight when inner city schools or known rivals were playing against us. Some games I made it to and other ones I had to work on. One that I did make on was when I almost got arrested. The game was against a school in the heights at a neutral location for a senate playoff game to determine who would go to the state tournament. It was a game that was about elimination toward going further to reach the State Championship Series of basketball games at the State Capital School arena.

We had been pumping each other up with the "ra ra" of who was going to do what school during the entire game. We had one the game, and they were heated. As soon as we started to get out of the out of town neutral arena, they started bombing on us, trying to hit us in the crowd, trying to sneak individuals who were not in the crowd, trying to leave the arena. We couldn't do anything but gather ourselves and start fighting back. The fight went out to the campus grounds of the university camp grounds. The university was only forty-five minutes to an hour away from my city. It wasn't the place for the championship and semi games, but it was an important event. Police came in big numbers to try and control things. I had just grabbed a rock to throw at one of the opponent students when I heard, "freeze drop the rock!" It was the police. They were right behind me. I just stopped right in my tracks. I was asked some questions but was let go when one of the school advisors—who was also a chaperone on the bus we came to the game on—had stepped in.

This wasn't the first time I got in trouble and the high school found out. They didn't find out everything, like my classmates and I using BB guns and shooting bus stops. I did get caught shooting a school friend—an underclassman—in the buttocks with the BB gun. We used to always do fake drive-bys. This time, it was on school grounds and the Spanish language teacher and my old homeroom teacher was driving right behind us. I was driving to school by my senior year, but I had let one of my classmates who lived around the corner from me drive while I did the shooting. As soon as my parents got home, I got the third degree of shame and questions of what and how I wanted to live life in the future. I was suspended for two days from classes but had to sit outside the principal's office both days. I am glad that I wasn't expelled.

This wasn't the first time that I was suspended from my high school. There was a food fight in the lunchroom, which had some good food. They served good hot cookies and donut cakes in the morning. So good that some of us used to sneak back down to the lunchroom and get some during homeroom. But anyways, it was a food fight that involved a lot of students. I was the only one who got caught and suspended for a day. Once again, I had to sit outside the principal's office during the school day. I was made an example because I tried to throw a small carton of chocolate milk to someone, but the carton was open straight from my lips. I wounded it up to throw, and the milk had spilled all on me. I guess they had to make me take the fall for it all since I was the one with the most evidence on me. Having to sit there outside the principal's office with females who came over from the school going coed, walking past and looking and even snickering, which really didn't bother me. My homey Gevis, who I used to go trick with, and I had a saying: "Fuck that bitch." It really stuck more after the school became coed. I mean, it was cool and all, but a lot of us guys still wanted to graduate under the original name of the school we started in. All we could say was that we were the first graduating class from the new name of the merged schools. It was our claim to fame, but we still wanted our original school name; it held more weight. Our school was known for a lot of good things and reputable people. The girls were cool and all. I had already known some of them from grade school and junior high. We used to always see different girls on the city bus. It was an interesting experience for that last year. I still miss it, just being with the bros. We had a connection at that school like no other. We would play the dozens in class, and the teachers would get involved like they were one of us just for a minute. We couldn't do that with the girls there.

I remember getting high off of marijuana on the way to the State Championship Game in basketball. Gevis and his older cousin had rented a car, and we traveled to the state capital for the game. It was about two to two and half hours away. My friend rolled up a joint. I think it was just one, but I was so high I was sweating. It was the first time I had ever gotten high. I had smoked before, but it was just for show. I was high as fuck. I showed up at the game chewed. Everything was funny, and then it was like I couldn't even stand and cheer for the game anymore. I had to sit down. Moments like that with the bros are the ones I will never forget. I had friends from school that used to come by my parents' house and visit. We were all close. During my junior and senior year, we basically all had some type of car to drive.

I had been driving since I was way young. My sister and I used to drive my father's work car. I was driving before I had a license. The hood used to pack in the ride, and we would joyride just to get a feel of being in a car with no adults. My sister and I used to share the work car to do different things. Once we got in an argument on the main street in the city. I was driving, and she wanted to go home, but I had one more stop to make.

She was like, "Take me home now!"

I said "Wait!"

She grabbed the wheel and turned it to make a left turn. I didn't know what to do. I couldn't stop her because she was strong that time. We almost crashed into a pole fighting over the wheel. We used to always get into fights. She was older and in college at that time. She acted like the world was all about her sometimes. I used to want to let her know that it wasn't. I learned later to just let her do her and I do me.

I always loved driving. I used to give rides for people to school. One guy from my neighborhood, a jerkish kinda hood homie named Sylvester, the "146 snitch that easily dropped on our music session" used to get rides from Hank and me. We split turns taking him when he went to our school. He wasn't really the best person to ride with. He was really goofy acting sometimes, and then sometimes he'd be cool. You never know what kind of person you get that day or for any given moment when dealing with Sylvester. One time, we both left him behind. He was basically from the neighborhood public school but transferred to our school; we had thought he did to follow us. I don't know what he transferred for. I guess a better chance at a known better school. He was a grade under us. We all repped the hood, but sometimes he repped the hood a li'l too strong for my taste. At that point in time, I learned everything wasn't always about the hood. There was a time and place for everything. I guess I was learning more how to be independent from my current surroundings and getting ready for real life or college and transition to turn my life into a real success. The hood was getting money. Everyone was driving and most had an extra show car besides what they were already sitting on. I had a li'l ride with mag-type rims, but I had heat in the trunk. Niggas said they couldn't always hear my words but always heard my bass coming from down the street. I wasn't a block boy, but I had some things as far as money bought, but I wasn't broke either. I was always getting forty ounces and kicking it.

Once my homeboy came by to treat me. He took me to some girl's house on the other side of the hood. We had a girl a piece. I had sex with mine in the bathroom. I had her suck my dick while sitting on the toilet. I placed her on the sink and fucked her real quick. Three days later, I was in the emergency room. I had tears like a motherfucka when I pissed. I was urinating razors, and then I had puss coming out of penis through the tip. I called off work and went straight to the emergency room. I didn't know anything about going to a clinic. I didn't even know where it was. While having sex with street girls, I was always strapped up with a condom, but since the homey Sylvester had set it up, I thought I was safe to have raw, unprotected sex. I confronted the jerk who set me up with the girl. He laughed and said, "Nigga, them was feemers!" I was like *What!* in my head. He could have told me before he set me up with the girl. I didn't know I was having sex with a crackhead, a fiend. I guess it was my fault anyways for letting the one homey who I had back for when we would be together but really didn't like being next to me because you could never know when he would try and do something inappropriate. Once when three of the hood homies and I walked down the street, he was with us, and the motherfucker pulled his penis out and started chasing us. A real jerk this guy was. He used to stalk females and would be looking through their windows but play it off as a joke or something. We used to have discussions about him all the time when he did stuff out of the ordinary. He always thought he was keeping some type of *G* code up from the streets and rap music and things. He was way too much on a lot of things. A real fucking jerk.

After, there was a surprising prom. I should have taken the girl Leslie from my job even though I was just her side boyfriend. I wish I could have taken her or my Bahama mama as the classmates called her my ex-girlfriend Shaniqua, whose junior prom I went to in my father's work car…LOL. I had that car shining and clean from inside out.

One of my friends from school came to the homie Hank's house down the street and saw me washing it and the finished product. He had said, "You spit shined that motherfucka!" He again yelled my last name, which was what a lot of my high school friends called me. "You can eat off that motherfucka!"

The junior prom was boring, but the kissing in the car at the neighborhood's recreational center parking lot was great. She had the sparkle from her lipstick on both of us. It was funny as I noticed it when I was taking her home. She was a grade older than me. I was thinking of getting myself together with more finances in my life when I dealt with her. I knew she could have been with any other older grade guy. I liked her so much that I stole a ring from my mother's jewelry box and gave it to her. I didn't think that my mom noticed the ring missing…come to find out it was one of my mother's most favorite and expensive rings. I had to chalk it up and go over there and ask for it back. I didn't lie to her about where I got the ring or whose it was, but I wanted to do it. I did lie to my mom, saying that I didn't know what had happened to her ring but knew that if Shaniqua came over with it on, I was doomed. My heart had started racing as my mom frantically searched for the ring. I knew I had to get it back. I didn't lie to Shaniqua and told her I was going to give her another ring but ended up letting her have my pager and red, black, and green African leather medallion and necklace. She was fine with that for the time being.

My high school friends used to call her Bahama mama. I used to think they were trying to start something. I just ignored them, but I would calm down to what they were saying because they always ended up saying she fine as a mothafucka too. It was just them playing the dozens. They really never could hate on her for real. I often thought of when she would go to college, how I would catch up. I wanted to get more money in my life, but I thought sticking to my promise to my father to not sell drugs and showing strength in character and succeeding in college would make me more on point with her. She brought that thought to me because she was older. I give her credit in my life for thinking of success, impressions, and responsibility of having enough or trying to earn enough to properly court a woman and live a good life with one. It could have been there before, but I give her credit for that strength of me in terms of impressions upon me in my life.

I found out later that she was keeping conversations and had thoughts of entertaining a guy with the same name—Sylvester—as my jerkish homeboy. Her homegirl told me this. I kept entertaining her homegirl, and we became close friends like brothers and sisters. I really never had any reason to not trust Bahama mama. Even though her beauty was a winner, she always showed and was willing to show love for me, and we always had good conversations and spent good times together. She told me she loved me before, and I told her the same. I guess hearing it for the first time was just a shock that I couldn't deal with, especially the thought of a guy named Sylvester. I also thought the jerkish fool had been lying to her and showing extra care for her to spite me and put her on his stalking list for sport. I saw Bahama mama one time after we broke up. She was so sexy and voluptuous that my mouth dropped when I saw her. It was at a high school college fair that was being held in my high school gym. She was so mature looking. I almost wanted to follow her around the whole damn place. Her titties were much more bigger, and her ass and hips were thicker. I mean, she was already fine anyways, but I was like "Goddamn!" She got thick than a motherfucka… The only thing I could think was she let some nigga fuck her and he matured her ass. My entire night was fucked up. She fucked my head by walking past, smiling, and speaking to me. I will never forget Bahama mama; I still think of her and have love in my heart for her.

After graduation, I got ready for college. I had chosen the school the others from my class didn't. I had chosen the state school where we had played state championship games at. Most of the others in my class were going to the school that was forty-five minutes to an hour away. That was the same place where I was yelled, "Freeze!" at by the police during a fight after a basketball tournament game. I visited them a couple times because their school started before mine did. Their school was on semesters and mine was on quarter-class schedules. It was wild there. I saw that they weren't going to be in the same dorm living facilities together for too long. They were having difficulties living with each other. They were having fun too, but the stress in the main room wasn't from the classes but from each other. I felt then that I was blessed to be going to a different school by myself. They would come in and out the dorm, and some almost got in fights. One of our friends did, but he was a member of the same gang I was affiliated with. The other guys were using that as an excuse to not get involved with helping him and not checking in on how things were with him. I was blessed by a high school homeboy Tamar, who was also a member of the Four Horsemen with me. I will always call him my OG in my regular talk with him, and I have no problem of seeing or hearing anything to deter me from thinking anything bad or internalized judgment from it.

I had not heard or seen the TV Man nor any spirits as I call them for giving me advice or learning. I had not seen or heard any illusions or hallucinations in years at that point.

The hood was already Crip from popularity of the block and our turf, friendship, and hood pride. I would give and get inspiration when I wore blue clothing. I noticed that. At first I thought it was because the other city side of the block school colors were blue and silver/gray. It was never any threat or *G* checking from my homeboys. Last thing I heard from them after graduation and leaving for school was one of the homies who got his car stolen by some cliques and gangs from the lower number streets was "He riding around like us!" I guess because I used to ride and bump music just to clear my head and feel free. My grandfather knew that that was my freedom from life. I was a rider. I loved to either drive or ride along and just vibe. It was a coping mechanism from the stress of growing up and all the mental torture that had happened in my life during that time. I had went from militant to accepting gifts from White girls. I went from seeing and hearing spirits and illusions to falling asleep in religious class, stemming from an education already awarded from grade school, to being peaceful with the neighborhood that once bullied and possibly abused me. I went from being under the house of a man and family that had to work lots of hours to where he got home from work, my sister and I would just stay clear of him so as not to get in trouble to leaving that household in hopes of starting a new life. Yes, the ride was my life and freedom. I was a rider for sure. I went from getting in trouble and being made an example of most of the times when caught to getting a basic education at a well-known school that could enable me for better things in the future. I went from being looked by both races as a burden and pride and looking in the mirror, seeing my right shoulder hanging lower than the left, thinking I was deformed, to believing I was touched by God and blessed for pulling through life so far and not giving up.

I made sure I stuck with my high school employment till my last scheduled days. I wanted something to be able to come back home to during breaks and have the ability to make income. I didn't want to call it as something to fall back on if I had failed in school, but it would have been a start of strong employment history. I had already made it to different positions during my high school time there. I even made it to interim upfront assistance manager that scheduled and administered breaks for baggers and stockers. I only graduated with a final 2.33 grade point average and had to start in the lowest levels of math and other classes. I didn't want it to hold me back. I was by myself, and all I had to do was settle and make do. I thought if I came in with an education with an active attitude, I wouldn't have a problem. I had already lost my car from an accident; I was in going to get my tuxedo for prom. So I shouldn't have no frustrations of the need to have extra money for gas and upkeep. I was getting a work-study job and just doing me to get a better life or an advanced chance to do so. My mental health was clear. I just knew I didn't have big money things to worry about. My student aid application was put in late, but my father paid my first quarter so I wouldn't have to wait till winter quarter and start in the fall. I thought I was ready for everything that would come. Well, I was prepared. I was about to endure and survive, and I endured and survived with many real events, stressful struggles, and abnormal events in my college life.

I was pumped to go to college. I was upset that I didn't have a car, but I was still motivated to make the best experiences that I could of my new adventures to come. My mother took me and my stuff down to the state capital school. It was a two-and-a-half-hour drive. It lasted three hours and twenty minutes because of all the students going down the same freeway. I really didn't talk much with my mother on that trip. I was more concerned about the traffic and her getting back home safely. I knew she might have wanted to discuss some things we had already been through at home a couple times months ago. I also didn't want her to worry or be sad that I wasn't going to a closer school. My sister went to a smaller school farther South than where I was going. So I wasn't too troubled about her going through the woes of her child leaving for school. I didn't want to say anything, act, or sound too wild in speech and say anything that would cause waves of disruption in the somewhat peaceful car. We just traveled to school with all my stuff.

Arrival at College and Start of Higher Education

I had my treasure chest of all my music with me. It was full of cassette tapes. I was a big hip-hop fan. I would go to the local record store almost, if not, every week. I got paid weekly from the job I was working during high school. I had damn near every hip-hop single and/or album that ever came out. I had the early years, like from the documentary movies of cyphers that were mainly local New York rappers, and I basically had everything since from all areas of the country, even my local city artist my homeboys would call "basement rap." I had my clothes and my li'l red desktop safe with the combination written on the bottom. I had some hygiene items and some extra money for books and supplies; other than that, nothing special.

My father had paid for my first quarter of school. My financial aid wasn't going to kick in until the winter quarter. I was to have a roommate in one of the dorms on the south side of the campus. I was supposed to pay my father back once my financial aid had kicked in. When it did eventually, I went to give the money to him to pay him back, but he didn't want it. I felt special 'cause I had some thousands to do with whatever I wanted. I was getting two grants that paid for the dorm rooms and three full meals during the weekdays and weekends. There was money left over for books and anything else that I could think of to make things more comfortable while in school.

When I first got to the campus and checked in, I had a first-floor dorm room. I didn't meet my roommate when I first went in. I noticed he had already been there. He chose the bed by the wall beside the doorway, where no one could look in walking past and seeing him. I had the window bed, but being on the first floor in the last dorm room by the stairs and the door outside, I didn't like. I didn't want anyone walking past and just looking at me whenever they wanted to, but I didn't feel right in changing the bed situation and didn't want to cause any problems.

My mother gave me her goodbyes and left. I am glad that it was quick because I wanted her to get back on the road, so she wouldn't be driving at night. It was fall, toward the end of September, and I think she could have gotten home right before dark if she had left right away.

She did, and as soon as she pulled off, I saw an upperclassman from my high school; his name was John B. He played football for the college, and he was in front of the building with some of his friends. I spoke with him and invited him to the room. When we got to the room, my roommate was there. I introduced myself and him. John B. asked me for some money. I was like, "Whoa!" at first, but he said he wanted to get a forty ounces, and I knew it wasn't that much for a forty ounce. So I gave him some loot, enough for about two forty ounces and some chips. He stayed and put me up on game about the campus, the people, the parties, the fraternity scene, and the history of the dorm I was in. The dorm I was in used to be an all-female dorm. The nickname for it was Straddle Me Hall. The dorm next to it used to be an all-guys dorm. Now they had mixed the dorms with guys on one floor and girls on the other, stacked up like that floor on top of another floor. It was good seeing big homey as my first Black person to actually see and talk to. He had graduated from our high school two years before I did. He was one of my high school friend's cousin. He was cool and funny. My roommate looked like he couldn't believe the language he was using when describing things. I guess my roommate didn't listen to much cursing and slang.

My roommate was cool though. He was White and looked like he was from the country or something. He looked like the White boys in the pictures with an all-blue jean overalls and a hay stem in his mouth. He was very smart. His education had surpassed mine as far as academics. His classes and schedule were that of an honor roll and mine of remedial. I never had a problem with him at first. One time, I was asleep, and I guess I was snoring because I woke up and caught him going back to his bed from my side of the room, like he had been looking at me sleeping or something. I don't know what he was doing and didn't question it at the time. I just knew that I didn't feel any touches, and my buttocks was cool. I was sleeping on my back, so I knew I was cool. I didn't know if he was gay or not. I just knew that he was polite. There's a big difference between being polite and being seen as gay or feminine, so I didn't want to yell at him at that time and claim him to be a faggot. I thought it was because I was snoring. I didn't make a big deal of it. He knew all the people that came to see me. They all introduced themselves, and I didn't mind talking to my family on the phone or friends in person in front of him. I mean, where else would I go? I did want to make big things out of things like that. Why make it uncomfortable for me and eventually the both of us?

There was a party every beginning of each quarter. They were called Icebreakers. All the Black people went to this party and the after-party. The parties were thrown by the fraternities and sororities. I had already met some new friends. They were all from different cities and some from my home greater city and the suburb, hood, or ghetto where I was from.

Once at one of the lunch tables in the cafeteria, I sat down, and there were two other Black guys there then three others went to sit with them. I had met the two already from my first day after John B. left my dorm room. I went walking around with another guy I met from Cleveland. He introduced me to some of the other guys that were in the dorms on the south side. Whenever he came to the lunch table and began eating, more introductions were done. A lot were from my home greater city and knew about my suburb city. They called it the hood and laughed. A girl came to the table and said she knew me. She started talking to me, and I remembered who she was. She was my OG Tamar's friend. I remember going to her house when

I used to pick him up, and we would run around visiting girls and stuff. She sat across from me, licking her ice cream cone and talking to me very nicely. We exchanged numbers and room numbers. One of the guys at the table was from South Central, Los Angeles. His name was Leonard; he said to the rest of the table that he couldn't hate and that he was impressed. I felt good when he had said that, especially with him being from LA and all. He was a big nigga and looked like he had been on some type of gang or street activity. Him and I became close really quick with the help of *Techno Bowl* and other video games. Later on, I found out he wasn't a gang member and didn't like the stereotype of it. He was a good student and a former college football player from another school out of state. He had gang knowledge due to the fact that where he was from, "you always have to know where you are at!" in his own words.

Well, it was time for another party. This wasn't the Icebreaker but just a regular party that they had every weekend. The main party hall was located on the south side. So we could just walk right to it. Me and mainly all the guys that were at the lunch tables would gather up and go. One time, we were walking to the party, and some White guys had tried to cut in front of us and bumped into us. We confronted them about that. They were acting like they had some type of right-of-way to do what the hell they felt like. One of the guys I was with started arguing more than the rest, and I thought there was going to be some blows thrown. I was the first to step up and have his back and the back of the group. I stepped up not to talk or argue between the main two but to throw blows. I don't know what came over me. I just knew it was time to do something and not get caught up in a surprise of them starting to swing or jump at us. The White boys saw I was about drama and calmed down. They walked away, and I was praised for about a week after that. It felt good, even though violence wasn't what I was there for. At least it was different from the hood where I had to basically win love just from being one of them after being bullied and all. This time, I showed faith to them that I had their backs and friendships started to grow. I mean, in the hood, I won respect more and more over time, but the older homies knew I would. It was like I just had to be around to put more work in. We fought with other schools, not hoods, when I was younger, and later the dope game was basically what the hood was about. I worked and sometimes hid dope for friends, but I wasn't banging and protecting the block like they were, but they knew I was down for our upbringing and friendship. Here at college, I was glad that I got that acceptance of having my new friends' backs quick, and any questions of it was over with.

My name was getting around that I had not backed down on the White boys. My name was also getting around because I was working a student financial aid work-study job. My name was getting around because I was from the same suburb as the deejays of most of the parties on campus and a dance group that aligned themselves with him. One time after a party that I didn't want to go to, I heard a girl I met who I had worked with from my job on campus walk past my window of my first-floor dorm room. She said, "One day I'm going to come by and get a look at those tapes you got!" I felt good about my decision to go to that school then. I got horny as fuck when I heard her say that. I wanted to fuck her li'l ass after she said that. I wondered who else knew I had tapes and what was going on with me.

There were so many Black girls at the school that I couldn't help but look at them when I was around them. There were all types. All from different parts of the state and different states. There were girls from cities in my state that I had never heard of. I would always wonder when I was going to meet someone or even if I should; I was still in remedial classes and had gotten cool with one female who was from my home greater city. She went to a Catholic school too, so it was easy for me to relate to her. Her name was Hope; she was in a freshman class that we, as freshmen, had to take during the first quarter of school. She stayed in a dorm area different from the south side. She was sexy and cute, but I didn't have the time to go over to where she was living in the dorms and communicate with her like I had liked to. She was a homegirl at heart but I believe smarter than me in the book game. I mean, my high school taught me a li'l bit, but I seemed to have had an education from other things. Everyone used to ask my opinion on things, and I gave it, and things just seemed to work out for the better from my advice. The facts of certain things, I didn't know. I just knew main concepts, feelings of underlying alternative issues, and ideas that I could break down and make points from and deliver them in either a shaming, neutral, or praising manner.

One girl I did get a chance to seriously be with was my OG's friend, and that time she was my new close friend I was interested in hooking up with. We weren't kissing or anything yet, but we would talk, and she would always hint on us getting together. Her name was Lola; she stated one time in front of my roommate when she came to visit that she was looking for a guy like me, someone she could talk to and feel comfortable with and didn't always ask for the cat!" I thought to myself, *If we were to get more serious like some of the other couples on campus, I would definitely be wanting to do much things to that cat.* I guess Lola didn't know my sexual history of tricking. She had a child at home, and I often wondered if we got serious, how things would turn out. Would I be finishing my education back home or become stepdaddy here in this city? My daydreams about her were rudely interrupted by a guy who I became friends with from my home greater city.

One time, the guy came by to see me before going to dinner. I was on the phone with Lola. When I got off the phone, he asked me what dorm she stayed in. I told him, but I thought he already knew, so I didn't think too much of it. He asked me what room number, but I didn't give it to him. We went to dinner, and then the next day, I called Lola but no one picked up the phone. I later heard that the guy—my new friend who had asked what dorm she stayed in—was asked to leave the school. I then found out that Lola went back home. I further found out two days later that he visited her in her room and tried to advance himself on her. She was so shocked and appalled that she had claimed sexual harassment from my understanding of things, but the rumor was that he raped her. Sometimes I would just sit and think of what happened in that room. I wondered how mannish he was. If he had pulled his penis out or was touching her or was strongly suggestive to the point where she felt uncomfortable. I never heard anything from Lola again. No goodbyes, no "I will miss you." All I know is that she was gone, and I had to continue doing what I was here for, which was school.

I felt that entire night that I should have told him to mind his damn business asking about her. I felt embarrassed because I didn't step up and couldn't be there to do anything. I felt silly because this was one of the same guys that I stepped to the White boys for and had their back, only knowing them for a couple weeks, but the one that I should have stepped up for was gone and was mistreated because I didn't step up and couldn't do anything. I felt foolish and mad that entire week. This guy was an upperclassman, and he was probably saying all kinds of mess to her. I was so heated that I didn't sleep that night when I found out. I often wondered what would OG say or want to be done about it. He was locked up. Tamar just got locked up on a murder charge. He made the newspapers and everything. I had to decide to just take care of myself and that everyone was not your friend just because they show a side for you and are friendly. That motherfucker knew that she was special to me and that we were being seen more and more together. I don't know why he would insult or have any wish to do anything like that. I often thought I was thinking too much about it but deep down knew I was right on point. I became bitter and bitter about niggas after that. I had gotten so bitter that during times at the Black Cultural Center, I used to just ignore and downplay what the pro-Black movement people were saying because I knew that they were all shady hoe-ass niggas deep down.

I had gotten cooler with the my LA homeboy Leonard. We used to go to the Subway food place and get subs at night. They had a special, always going on two for the price of one. I used to pay because I had income from my work-study job. I know what they mean by the "freshman 15." We would go damn near every night there. Except Tuesdays, that was "wing night." Back then wings were only twenty cents on Tuesday at BW3s. There were a lot of bars and food places on the main street on campus. One time, a bunch of us went to Subway, and when I got inside, there was a nigga, a bum or something, in there who started getting loud. He started trying to rank on me about my size. He had called me a fat boy. I don't know what came over me; I just started beating him in the head so fast and so many times I was like a madman. I was hitting him all with my right arm and fist, swinging over and over and over again. When I was done, he had li'l birdies going around his head like the cartoons. I mean, he was still sitting in the chair but barely. He was moving his head and upper body in a circular motion, like he was just trying to hang onto his consciousness. One of the guys I came with said I had knocked him out and back into consciousness. They all couldn't believe that I had snapped so fast. I don't even remember saying any-thing to the guy, no yelling at him or nothing. I just turned around and stood in line to order my sub. One lady there said that it was a shame what I had done to him, and I should be ashamed of myself. I didn't say anything; I just stood in line, waiting to order my sub. The guys I came with were all shocked. There was an awkward silence, then one of them said he just beat the fuck out that motherfucka as he put his head down with his hand over his face. I don't know if it was or not that others wanted to compare themselves to me, but ever since then, there was a difference in the way people had looked and talked to me. It was always like they were trying to prove some-thing or get a point across to me for agreement. I was always getting approached about pro-Black issues.

I had my own dorm room by the spring quarter. My old room-mate and I had no quarrels, but I think the differences started to take a toll. I could notice him getting irritated by my company coming by when they would come from classes. The convenience of the side door and the stairway to the upper floors always had them coming by for a minute. A couple of them would talk to him nasty and rude like. I was embarrassed, and it wasn't because he was a White boy, but I could notice a change starting to come from him. He didn't say anything. He didn't have to. It was his demeanor and small attitude during the hours when company would usually stop by. I wanted to talk to him about it, but I just filed for another room that had opened on one of the upper floors. It was a single room and was down the hall from my LA homeboy. I used the fact that I had seen him leaving from my side of the room when I was asleep as a motive for the move in my request. I told them that I thought it was because

I was snoring, but I didn't think that it should have happened. I guess I was wrong in what I was trying to say but didn't fully feel wrong at heart asking for the request. I didn't care though. He was cool and all, but if I wanted no problems in my new school conditions, then I had to do what I had to do. I worded the filed request, not to mentioning him in any physical wrongdoing but just that I felt uncomfortable.

Other Blacks on campus used to be righteous about being pro-Black, but I felt that they were fraud. They all preached of being pro-Black, which is cool, but they were doing the same things that they said they were against. The fraternities and sororities would all get pro-Black movement but then would be fighting or about to fight either on campus during classes or at the weekend parties and Icebreakers. I listened and learned a lot more about the facts and people during the different eras in history from just the talk and lectures of the pro-Black awareness on campus. One example of being pro-Black to me was not to associate formally with White people, just speak and keep it moving. Don't interact violently unless approached and you have to defend yourself. I always thought that and that was what was being preached, but one night, my eyes opened up to a different meaning. I mean, the Four Horsemen and I used to beat up the White fellow classmates in high school, but we still had love for them. It was something that was associated with our school, and we are all still friends and growing friends with the same White guys till this present day.

One night after drinking forty ounces of beer, we went walking on campus. The first White people that we had seen, a couple of the guys just started bombing on them, hitting and spitting on them. They were claiming that they were doing it for revenge for all the slave years. I didn't get a chance to hit one of the White boys, and I am glad that I didn't. I played it off, saying, "Man, as soon as I tried to jump in, y'all was done!" I didn't want to get involved hitting the White people, but I also didn't want to seem too distant from being a part of the crowd. One of the guys caught a White boy with a couple of his friends by the Black cultural center, which was also located on the south side. The White boy's friend ran, and the White boy was there solo; he had a Walkman that was ripped from him. He was beaten to the ground, and one of the guys I was with named Charles stepped on his face. I mean, he had not only stepped it, but he jumped and landed on his face. That was when I knew to get away from the crowd before the police came. Fortunately, that was the same thing everyone had thought. They praised what was done that night for about two weeks. It was in the school newspaper, but no one was ever caught. It seemed that timing had got my back. I wasn't seen as a coward or a traitor of the self-proclaimed pro-Black movement. I was though. I didn't agree with going out that night; I would rather have slept in.

I started to get tired of niggas at that point. My attitude after that wasn't horrible, but I wasn't impressed with the Black awareness on campus and started seeing the Black folk on campus more and more differently. I started to despise them more than the time from when my Hope girlfriend-to-be was rumored to have been raped. I went there to go to school and make a change for myself. Even though I had been involved in couple incidents already, I really felt justified and thought things I had done was expected. This, I didn't. I felt like if I didn't see them differently that I would get in big trouble for some Black people I really didn't even know. I didn't feel like a sellout and wasn't considered one because of a small white lie and timing, but I didn't feel like one anyways because I was from a Black community and city, and I felt they didn't come from and didn't go through the same things that I have. Some of those guys were from small White communities, and I thought they were just letting off steam from a struggle that I didn't think they hadn't fully experienced yet. Who am I to say that though? They didn't know my past just like I didn't know theirs. Everything was all assumptions of each other, and I thought that that wasn't enough to do major jail time or get expelled from campus just because the crowd wanted to go live and do some silly shit. I saw them as if they couldn't compare to me. I felt like I should keep a li'l more distant if I could and not act funny when I was around them in a group and to just be cautious of them.

I started to notice that my new friends and associates were starting to think that I was having too much or had the ability to get and do things. It was like they would all huddle up and say, "We go get him today." One time while in my dorm room, which I was always smoking weed in—I don't know why I was smoking drugs while on federal state property, but the floor supervisor didn't seem to mind. He never came and said anything to me. Everyone knew I was getting and smoking weed. Girls used to come by and guys too. I had a Sega video game. We used to play games like *X-Men* and other games. Down the hall, Leonard from LA had a Sony, and we played football on his. I had finally got a sports game for the Sega, and everyone started to come more and more to my room. A guy from my suburb city came by; he had went to our city's local high school. He was older and an upperclassman, but I heard he was flunky. The campus had a bunch of flunkies on it. Flunkies were those who stopped going to school but still used to hang on campus and try to be around campus activities. He came by and left quick like he had just come to check things out. I felt kinda funny and checked my things when he left. I had noticed that one of my tapes was missing. It was my Bushwick Bill cassette. I had gotten so mad that I started to kick everyone in the room out. I knew the guy was a flunky, and I probably wouldn't see him for a while. They seemed to come around and then disappear sometimes. Another guy from my neighborhood who was a younger student by a year had tried to calm me down. I don't know if he just didn't want to leave the room and continue to play the video games and listen to music or not, but I still wanted everyone to leave. I was pissed. That was when I thought I started to become more paranoid of Black people and people from my own city. I could expect that from someone who was from another city but from someone to come from my home city and not show love or do some deceitful type of shit had me heated and untrusting of people who came like they were cool 'cause we had something in common. It was like he was a "get in where you fit in" type of nigga. I was told to not trust those kinds because they are stressing, fitting in for some bullshit reason. It is just like when Black people talk down on other nationalities or Colors of People, and they are loud with it while talking to me. I always hated that. Just because you have an issue, don't add me to your side like it is my problem too, embarrassing me in front of those people who until that point, I didn't have a problem with.

I did have friends from the neighborhood visiting that I grew up with, and my trick buddy from high school, Gevis, would come from time to time. One time, damn near the whole city came down. We were all in the dorms smoking, and they were coming in and out of the room. There were so many homies that a few of us slept in my friends' cars. When the weekend was over, I had nothing but cigars inside and beer bottles all over the carpet floor in my dorm room. My father came to town and surprised me with a visit. I had to clean up all that mess by myself while he watched and asked questions of how the room got that way. I mean, there were so many cigars inside from rolling blunt after blunt. It was amazing that I didn't get kicked off of campus, or school for that matter. The guys on my floor were cool though. They never called in on me, plus they partied too. They would get wildly drunk and get crazy at times. I never called on them, so I guess we were all like family with our li'l floor secrets.

One friend from the neighborhood came down not just to kick it but to go to school. It was that motherfucker Sylvester who I thought was a jerk at times but other times pretty cool. He came down, and he had a car shortly after being there. I was upset when he came because it was like, "Damn! First he followed me to high school and then he followed me here." This is the same MF who Hank and I used to give rides to school to when he went to our school for a short period, before he got kicked out. We both left him one day. It was a real annoyance to ride with him sometimes, but his mother paid us. You never know what level he was on.

Mixing School with Street Life and Off-Campus Living

He came to the campus, and I didn't treat him badly. I showed love for him when he almost got jumped, and I even went to ride on some niggas with him. We were in his car, a box burgundy Regal. We went to a store in a neighborhood close to campus, but it wasn't a part of the university. While inside, I heard one of the local niggas go in and say to his boys that were already in the store, "Get the nigga in the Sox hat!" which was Sylvester. We were on guard when leaving. At first I didn't see no one, but when we got in the car and pulled off, they started throwing bottles at us. Sylvester was pissed. I was just like, "Damn!" wondering what the fuck was up with the niggas, what made them trip on us or him. I just knew he did something there before for them to act like that. Why did the dude go in and say just get him and not both of us. I just knew this jerk-ass nigga did something earlier to them. It seemed as though he had to for them not to try to get both of us. I thought maybe he tried to talk or flirt with one of the neighborhood females and things went sour or something. Knowing Sylvester, he probably had some drug activity going on with them or was just high, siding on them like he was way more boss than them. Riding past, dogging them in the way of hitting corners or even throwing up the hood gang sign to them—something along that line. I had a hat on too. Why they didn't say get the two niggas were in the hats, it had to be something.

A couple weeks later, he came by the room and picked me up with another guy who was a freshman. They wanted me to ride and handle some niggas who had tried to jump him earlier. They were from the same area where the bottle throwers were from. I didn't know until we started riding and we were in the same area. I was thinking like, *Why would the nigga go back over to the same area where niggas definitely didn't want him over there?* That was the hood, in my opinion, plus we were supposed to be down there for school. I was in the passenger seat and was the suggested shooter. I had a hoodie on but didn't have the hood part over my head. We rode and didn't see anything or anyone. Then we started coming back toward campus and was going to do another sweep through the hood. When we got the main street that started the campus and where all the bars and lights of the scenery were on, I saw the police. I had put the hood part of my hoodie on my head but didn't pull it tight. I did it just in time, and since I didn't pull it for them to think we were suspicious, they didn't suspect anything. They had their hands full, but they could have called some other cops to look out for us or, even worse, say I was to start dumping on the niggas and a description was given. I could have been more easily proven with intent because I had tried to hide my face while on the seek to attempt.

The freshman driving said, "What did you do that for!"

My hood homeboy Sylvester said, "Now that was smart!"

I guess he was thinking the same way I was. He always had an eye on me. We had fun growing up the hood, but I noticed he always had an eye on me and was always a li'l friendlier than the other guys in the hood with me; it seemed as though he was a li'l extra though. I think since he was used to watch me, it automatically put me on guard. I think he knew that. Another hood homey, Tom, who also had concerns and talked about him to me in the past, told me that his mother used to make him read the Bible every day! I thought power when I first heard that, like the God Supernatural commercials. I didn't want part of his thinking. No, I didn't want part of his noggin! I just thought to myself after hearing that. I felt he had the power to conjure and see that his hexing was justified by the good book. I felt he could use the Bible as a weapon. I always was leery of his behavior. This is the same guy who pulled his penis out and chased us down the street back in the days.

Well, we didn't find the niggas. I once again felt like having the back of my friends, but I felt funny by what the driver had said. I felt that he tried to treat me like I was a sucka or a poo butt or something, like I had never used a gun or been in any trouble in my life before, like I was a straight nerd or some shit. I felt that nigga was a bitch for thinking that. Then I thought the way that Sylvester was perched up in the back seat and chillin' like he was some type of OG, I thought they was about some game or something. I felt that they had tried to get me involved in on their bullshit and, at my expense and my college career, would be the one in trouble for them. That was they beef, but I was in the shooter position while they judged me. I became more untrusting of how people would get when involved with me. Either I was seen as a pushover, or they really needed my help, but they weren't new to any hood activity or violence either. The more I thought about it, I felt like there were more of some fuck niggas than what I first thought. They probably would have just blamed me if I was to dump on them city niggas and we got caught. I was supposed to take the downfall or be considered a hoe-ass nigga if for not keeping the G code that they wanted to hold me to.

Later on in the dealings with my hood friend and being down at school, it became apparent that I should disassociate myself with him. One time while back home on a break from school, he and I had gotten a sack of weed to smoke. I opened the bag to break down the sack. The motherfucker leaned over and looked back to get my attention from him and what he was really doing. I saw the motherfucker pouring some fluid in the sack.

I told him I didn't want it. I said, "If you wanna have the sack to yourself, that bad here!"

He got out the car and started directly complaining a couple times, saying, "Why you don't want to smoke wit me!" With his whining voice getting more and more annoying 'cause he thought funny like a female.

That's why he was whining was all I could think as rode off. Then I thought he was just on some shit, trying to get me on some pookie shit, trying to slip me something while he was around so he could try something or have me in a fucked-up situation looking fucked up like a motherfucker.

I guess he didn't think I was G enough and wouldn't notice. I mean, I had been into fights and did things that he and other homies in the hood didn't know about. They were doing their own thing. He was the only one always questioning niggas' G status. I mean, he did street activities and was still about certain things but ain't nobody stupid and just let you do what the fuck you want to do with them. The ultimate code to me was there was no code. It was about manhood at that point. Really earlier than that but definitely at that point 'cause the jerk-ass nigga tried to hate on me hard and got caught because I was keeping it realer. I was never in the mood to try things on others like that. That is some sucka soft-type shit. The type of shit bitches do to get you as slick without you trying to prevent them and beating on their ass.

I guess he felt me switching on him, but I was at school. I was the same homey who rode for his ass to take a penitentiary chance just because he was a homey from the hood. As I kept pulling away from him more and more, I started to talk more negative of him. We always talked negative about him back home, even though it was all jokingly done and right in his face. I started like that when he first got there; it was just a way we were in the hood. Maybe with me acting like he was a bother, maybe he wouldn't have been. I always saw different sides to the way things came from and would be about.

One time, he walked in on me when someone had asked me a question about him. I told the truth about him, which had him looking bad. The way he put it was like I had always been putting him down, but actually that was the first time. It wasn't any language or rhetoric to show love from a hood basis. I guess all the feelings of how I thought he was a jerk for real had to come out. When it happened, I was in one of the girls' room who all lived in one of the triple-bedroom dorm room at the end of the hallways.

After that, I still talked to him when he came around. He had been living off campus with an African friend of mine named Huko, whose family where partially from the United States and the other half from Africa. It was an off-campus place, but Huko was sharing a place with his girl. He felt sorry for Sylvester, I guess. My hood homie brought drama to his house. He tried to steal in front of me and even asked me to reach and give what he wanted to steal to him. I told Huko later what I was asked to do after he and Sylvester had fallen out. I didn't want to be known like that. My home city already had a bad reputation as being a city that thugs and drug dealers were from. I was always asked, "I heard your city got nothing but schemers and thieves and couldn't be trusted!" Now he was bringing that stereotype to life. Since he still used to go around me, everyone thought I was on bullshit too and couldn't be trusted. He gave the hood and the home city a bad name. He wasn't the only one, but he was the main person closely connected to me because we actually grew up together.

The police came to Huko's house because of Sylvester. The way Huko told me, it made Sylvester seem to be a helper for the police. The way it was explained that my hood homey came running in the house from police and went straight to the closet, where Huko had a small plant of marijuana at. The police then came in after him and also went to the closet, but directives were changed to questioning my friend Huko about what was in his closet. They stopped looking for Sylvester and didn't even question him or his whereabouts. It was so simple to see that he was a snitch of some sort. In fact, Huko was the first person to tell me that. I told him that he might have done it to get revenge, and then Huko quoted a rapper, "A snitch is snitch!" I didn't hear from Huko for a while after that. We had gotten close because we were on the same pledge line for a Black fraternity. My hood homey Sylvester had disappeared for a while too. I don't know if he went home and went to jail or if he had gotten a place in the city where the college is. I did hear that he was back at home doing his thing again later.

I had moved from campus and had gotten an apartment close to campus. It was walking distance directly to the south side of the campus before the middle of the campus had started. I had a roommate named Lavar. He was another friend, who at one point in time was on line trying to join the fraternity with me. He was older, two grades higher than me. He was from New York, but it wasn't the main city New York, New York. He was cool, but he put on the New York accent on a li'l too much for some people. I thought it was just hip-hop talk. He was really big on local New York artists, which at this time were always coming out with songs in the stores. He also had local New York artist and deejay mixes that he would let me hear. Some people used to call him a pseudo New Yorker and a fake nigga 'cause they thought his accent shouldn't be like from the actual city of New York.

The apartment was nice a two-bedroom with a crawl-in storage area located off the dining area next to the kitchen. We had basic college furniture, and I bought a waterbed from Lavar's best friend, who was also from my greater city hometown. He had other friends I met who were students on campus and another school in the city. They both were from my home state but two different cities. I kicked with them before smoking bud at Lavar's and his best friend named Greg's old apartment. We all got high. I used to get high as fuck and keep on smoking. They used to stop before me back then; there were no such thing as reggie or mid grade and loud and gas. The determinations were college good weed and city garbage weed. There was a weed man who used come by, a White boy who had all kinds of different weeds. I tried skunk for the first time in their old apartment. I got the connect for the White boy for myself. I was a great customer. I worked, and that money was extra for me. My grant money took care of my rent and bills, plus with me being a student, I got full amount of allotted food stamp benefits. It was about $200 per month.

School classes were going good. I liked seeing the people and the girls on campus, so I went to class. Any other time I was on campus at work or at the apartment smoking and drinking with my roommate, listening to east coast music. I still had my choice of music that I was listening to and all my tapes from high school. CDs were starting to come out and was still purchasing music. I had a mixture of music that I listened to now. Groups like Mobb Deep, I hadn't heard of before, and deejays like DJ Clue and doo-wop were great to listen to and gave me a fulfillment of underground hip-hop different from *MTV Raps* or *Rap City*. I was listening to groups like 5th Wards Boyz and Too Much Trouble. I also had solo artists that I love, like Brotha Lynch Hung, but I was deemed as being too gangster and in need of refinement. I had all kinds of music on deck, but that gangster shit was always my favorite. When my neighborhood friends were listening to east coast back in the days, I was listening to underground artists and groups from my city.

One of my friends back then called it "basement music," trying to talk down on it, but I used to bump it constantly. I went from listening to east coast at a very early age and being ridiculed by my father, calling it shit, to listening to west coast, south, and local underground artists like Raw Ice Dynasty, and it being called garbage or basement music. I didn't care; it was my style. I love hip-hop and gangster music. Some were upset with me on campus because my pants were still sagging. I guess I didn't conform enough for them. Fuck 'em, I ain't give a fuck about what they thought, and I think they knew that. I already had gotten more pussy and head than those motherfuckers from tricking and regular girls. I didn't care what they thought. I listened to them just to get an idea of where they were coming from.

My friend from LA who was also on the line for the fraternity with us for a period of time would come through. He asked me one day if I cared about life. I told him I was more concerned how my mother would feel if I had died! I really didn't care about life too much. He was so surprised and serious when he said I needed Jesus. I thought he was starting to get corny on me but respected his point of view since he was from LA and all. I was working, going to school, and I used to carry a firearm everywhere I went. No one messed with me anyways, but I was always prepared with my .380 semiautomatic handgun that was filled with hollow tips and one in the head. I didn't think my behavior was bad for him to ask me that, but I guess he was either being a comedian or maybe he saw something in me. I didn't see how he was going with those conclusions about me just from conversation and jokes about things and events we would either talk about or see on TV.

I respected his opinion on things, but enough was enough. At least he was learning the real me. Maybe I did need Jesus at that point in life, but I didn't see me needing him. I didn't even fully believe in the guy, and I had questions of his concepts that helped promote white supremacy, in my opinion. The turn-your-cheek aspect was a little too much for me to agree with. I felt it was in the good book to prevent Africans from rebelling or letting White folk do what they wanted to with them. I was still militant, thinking just because I wasn't wearing red, black, and green like X Clan, doesn't mean I didn't have Black love. We then marched with X Clan to and from downtown of the city from south side of the campus. I know that doesn't make me a member of any official movement, but it might be because nothing else was done after that. I didn't start things on campus or in the city.

Most people and friends were just upset because I was smoking weed strong, and my real active business wasn't out there being judged wrongly. But it started to with living with Lavar. He had so many questions and then would throw the answers back at me like he knew me or something.

I had listened to different kinds of music on deck. I used to make mixtapes to listen to while walking and being on campus. I used to shut the world out and avoid all the things that might have been there as far as questioning if my sagging pants or wondered why I didn't finish joining the fraternity I started to join. I was on a mission to get my GPA up, which I messed up from pledging. I had dropped line, and I didn't care of the trip they put us on. We were doing all the necessary activities, but their chapter was suspended.

They didn't even want to let us know about that, but we were at fault too. Some of us didn't have the GPA that was needed to join. Some of us were short by just a point number or so. We all wanted to do it together for the brotherhood, and some just said that they were going to go along with our plan to join but were really going to leave the rest if we got caught in our trickery. We manipulated the system, or at least we thought. We had changed the transcripts to show that we all had high-enough GPAs to finish the process of joining. The transcripts looked awful. They were way off color, and the lining of information was a little off, but we thought it would work. It didn't, and if it did or not after we learned that they were being questioned but might pass through. We found out that they didn't have an active chapter, and it was to be put on us to pay the reinstatement fee of over two thousand dollars before we could join.

They never told us that during any meetings or at any time we were running around and in study sessions, and they definitely didn't tell us after I got dropped to the ground one night from getting hit in the head with a frying pan. They definitely didn't tell us after all the wood we took to the ass in the name of unity and tradition for the frat. All the ridicule and exercising for nothing. I even wore a garbage bag with Vaseline inside of it on my bare skin to lose weight to join the motherfucker. I wore it in classrooms and everything! Getting totally embarrassed, thinking it would pay off with glorified membership. Yep, I didn't give a fuck what others had to say about whatever dealing with me after that. It seemed as though life was just making sure that I went in with the same attitude that I said I needed to have and thought I had from my first day arriving to college.

A lot of us had quit. I didn't quit till after I fell from getting hit in the head with a frying pan. They had me sit on the side and calm down and then wanted me to start doing push-ups. I told them I had a heart problem, which I did, and they excused me. I went to Leonard's apartment the next day. He had recently stopped. He stopped because of the fact that they didn't have an active chapter. He and some of the others went through the same thing the year before. He was fed up and wanted to concentrate solely on graduating. I was down for the same thing. He spoke of going to Freaknik. I had heard of it but wasn't sure if I wanted to go.

The local Icebreakers were cool, but this was in Atlanta, Georgia. And it was a lot of prep to do, and I wasn't sure I would be able to get all the money like I wanted to have to do something like that. We quickly turned the conversation to not being considered or letting the light of being an eternal *lampada* to the fraternity get to us. If things were all the way legit and us ourselves being all the way legit with our grades, it would have been all good. We just didn't stop just because we couldn't take it or was weak or scared. I've been wanting to quit, but I didn't want to be seen as a quitter by the campus bruhs and my older friend from my neighborhood Keith, who had wanted me to grab his belt before entering the doors of the high school the first day.

He was a bruh at a different school. I knew he was going to visit soon and was going to tear me up either with jokes and hits or jokes and wood. I was ready for him, but the noncare of the bruhs on the campus from me, damn near getting knocked out and my head split open with a frying pan, and the nature of stability of us even being legal put more of a determination of me stopping.

I had been known on campus for a couple reasons up to me pledging already. I started to hang less with the guys and was carrying a strap after I stopped pledging into the fraternity. I met a girl in the dorms named Lisa, who I had seen a couple of times on campus and spoken to. I wasn't living on campus but went through the south side of campus from time to time to see the girls that worked at the front desk of my old dorm. We were cool and we were always kidding around. Lisa had walked past, and I went to her floor shortly after talking to my front desk lady friends. I saw she was in her room. I didn't know which one or which floor she stayed on. I was just cruising the hallways. I still had lady friends that stayed in the building that I would talk to over the phone and go visit. I started talking to Lisa while in her doorway. She was willing to give me her number, but I didn't call her right away because the next day, I saw her walking down my street my apartment was on, and she was walking and talking to some guy. It was like they were going to his place to fuck. That was the only thing that I could think of, so I said to myself that I would wait to get in contact with her.

There were plenty girls that came by the apartment I had with Lavar, the pseudo New Yorker, as most of the in-state niggas called him. He had plenty of girls he knew from his freshman year. He had been in school longer than me. We would smoke, and some of his friends would come by, and they would jump in the storage area off of the dining room and get high as fuck in the small space. I could never fit in there. I never tried and didn't want to. I didn't want to embarrass myself getting in and out of that motherfucker. They used to ask me and encourage me to go in, but I never did. I told them, "You not finna embarrass me, and I'm not finna embarrass myself!"

We used to kick it hard, but I smoked more than them. It seemed like I smoked more than everyone, which is one thing I was known for.

We used to work during the summers with youths from across the state. We had training, and this was the second year for me. This was the first time I had been working on the summer from an off-campus apartment. I worked the previous summer on campus in the program, but I didn't have my own apartment at that time; I was still in the dorms. After my first year of school, I worked as a temporary employee at the post office. That post office job was with my homeboy Gevis's mother. This summer was different because it was hotter than normal. Having a place to stay on and off campus was a good thing. We had to stay on campus because that was the program policy to work with the kids, but having a place to go to was neat, so I thought. It never happened to be that way. Lavar and I lost the apartment. He was extremely funny acting when it was time to take care of business. We had issues in the toilet of the apartment, and he didn't want to pay his portion of the rent because of it. I paid my portion, and my mother had cosigned the lease on my behalf. When it was time to go to court, I was ready to go, but he hadn't even gotten dressed yet.

Waiting on him, I would have been late; in fact, I was but one of his old friends and my new friend Edward came by and offered to take me to the courthouse. I was embarrassed to say that I was representing our living arrangement. I found out from the judge that Lavar had used a false cosigner and had misspelled his name on purpose so that he would not be liable to pay. Even though I had a work-study job, I didn't have a total amount of what they wanted for back rent for him and the little remaining rent. My mother had to pay the court bill. I was pissed but knowing him and his siked New York way of things, dealing with him was a scam. We had good times in that apartment, but I was really suspecting of him from that time on.

In that apartment, I learned to always have my hair washed. I had good hair, especially in the back, like my father. My head would itch, and I had a lot of dandruff. When I washed it, my hair would curl up, and I wanted to play the curly hair, and I would play with it and twirl it. Some used to play the dozens and say they were li'l curly kookabugs or naps, but the girls would always give me compliments. Once I was sitting in my favorite chair in the living room, and I used to scratch my head to relieve the dandruff. I did know that I was leaving the dandruff on the top back part of the chair. I came home from class and was told by Lavar that I was a nasty motherfucker in front of his friends. I was more understanding than embarrassed. Another time I was supposed to be embarrassed was when I was making some mixtapes for me to walk to while on campus. I drunk some MD 20/20, the blue kind. Actually, I had goosed it. I was sweating but having a good time buzzed out of my mind making this tape. I always stuck to the rule of "no breaks, no time" for a commercial to fit in between songs. Some city girls came over and were flirting with guys in the room. I was asked a question about something silly, and I answered it, but two of the girls had repeated what I was saying sarcastically, I thought. My attitude changed so quick they had gotten quiet and couldn't enjoy their little remark. I guess they saw the expression on my face or felt stress from me. I ignored them all the rest of their visit. I learned that all people want is some attention in a way where they would be the victor. I felt like the victor in that situation.

I had company too; my homies from the hood came down a couple of times during that year. One time, one of my homeboys, Jabral, asked to use my gun while he was here. I felt funny when he asked, but he provided a little pressure. I let him use it. Lavar, who always had something to say, said that I was wrong for doing so. He further stated that he could be out there doing anything. He then said, "You know them boys where you from sell drugs and be in gang violence!" I sat and wondered where he thought that from and why he was stereotyping my friends.

I never told him that they sold drugs or that they were gang-banging. I never said that this one particular homeboy who he had never met sold drugs or did anything. It did stick to me what he said though. I wanted to ask Jabral for the gun back, but I didn't want to go and find him. I wasn't worried about what he was doing with it. I just wanted to make sure I got it back. He wasn't down there to do some dirt or anything. He was visiting a female he met from coming to a campus block party from a previous year. He didn't want to travel dirty, so he asked to carry mine to feel more protected. I knew what it was and didn't appreciate my roommate getting in or speaking on my business. It wasn't his business what we were discussing or in transaction about, if it was done in his presence or not. I asked Jabral for the gun back before he caught the bus back. He felt funny about it, but I was naked too. So he had no choice but to give it back since I was due to go back on campus from my apartment the next day after the weekend. I am glad I got it back too.

One time while walking home from classes and work, I was almost assaulted and robbed. My gun was the only thing that scared them away. I didn't even hear them walking behind me, but I felt something. I had my music up loud in my headphones and my books and gun in my backpack. I didn't know what they were interested in. It could have been my bag with books for them to cash back in at the campus bookstore or if it was the gigantic headphones I wore even for that day and age in technology. I felt them coming, but I didn't hear them. I slowly started to take one of my shoulders from under the straps of my book bag. I zipped my bag open and grabbed the strap. I stopped and turned around and showed the strap extended in my hand down by my side. I saw two older men—one a Black man dressed in all blue with a blue gang rag tied around his head. The other was a White man who was wearing all red and a red gang rag tied around his head.

Once I had the strap out on the side, away from me, they jetted through the closest apartments they could find. I chased and fired in the air in the back of the apartments. I told my friends about it later and got different reactions. Some asking if I was okay and others just saying that it was a shame. Lavar was the only one with a simple reaction of "Word!" with his silly fake New York accent having ass. I don't know if he and my homeboy who had come down and asked for the gun had something to do with it or not. While they were in the same room, I overheard someone say, "Well, what do you want, a sickness from the White race or harsh reality from your own!" I took the meaning as the White man in red was a sickness of the blood in most Black people's system and system of raping us Black folks over the years and the Black man in blue as the inner color of blood in the body, but the harsh cold blackness you come across when dealing with your own kind sometimes. Some say most times.

I had female company in the apartment too. I had much fun with a couple of girls in there. A couple where prostitutes. I had some come by when Lavar went out of town. He left an old-school caddie and said I could use it. I went kicking it on the other side of town. I had sex in his car with a couple girls, one of them in the back seat of his shit. I brought one back to the apartment. She was okay in the looks, but she was willing to go the full round for like $30. I fucked the shit out of her. She came while riding me backward with her ass to me on the floor in the living room. I didn't want to take her upstairs to the bedroom. After she busted a nut, I got on top, still with the rubber on. I didn't bust a nut yet and started to stroke inside her. She was so active with it you would think I would have come, but I didn't; I had faked one. She said, "How do you do that!" I just got up and acted like I didn't know what she was talking about. I thought she had known that I faked an orgasm. I didn't care to explain to her. I just dropped her back off.

I had another prostitute I caught on while I was walking. I had walked eight streets over to find her. I would walk to a block and wait to see who I could see walking. I would approach them and ask them to come to the apartment. All of them were down until they found out how far we had to walk. I guess they didn't want to go for the forty-dollar price I was offering or maybe they felt unsafe walking with me by themselves. I don't know what was on their minds, but I know I didn't want have sex outside in the open. I met a girl; she was thick as fuck. She looked like a Black-and-Puerto Rican mix. She was willing to walk back to the apartment but only for sixty dollars. We got to the apartment, and I took her upstairs. I thought she was worth it. Her body was so perfect and she was cute. She gave me head, and I got on top and stroked in her and kept stroking. I busted a nut, and when I got up, she was rubbing her pussy and looking at me with her face squinted. I should have grabbed another rubber and talked her into more time for free. About two weeks later, she showed up on the doorstep with a six-pack. I had company from the next building over. We were playing *Madden*, and I was embarrassed because of how I met her. I didn't let her in, and she was upset and cursing at me through the door.

Prostitutes weren't the only girl company I had. My friend Leslie from back home came to visit. She had her baby, and it looked like it could have been mine. She sent me pictures of him, and he looked like a little teddy bear. The baby resembled both of us because she was very cute and attractive. Her skin was milk chocolate and so was his. They both looked adorable to me in the picture. Her for her feminality and him because the picture was of him still as a toddler holding a teddy bear. She came with my neighborhood friend Hank, who was visiting a female lover who went to my school. Leslie didn't smoke, but I smoked downstairs with Lavar and the other guys while she waited upstairs. She drove and I was glad that I didn't have to worry about picking her up from the bus stop and all that mess.

We were upstairs and having fun, and I felt her split the tip of my penis with her tongue. I never felt that before. It stung a li'l bit. We were doing us, and then I started eating her out after I had busted a nut. I saw that she was feeling it, but I got tired. I guess all the smoking did a number on me. I started playing with her clit with my finger. I didn't want to put my fingers inside of her. I never thought that girls really liked that. I always felt funny about just poking it up in there. I didn't want the girls to say, "Ouch!" or get a bad feeling about me sexually as being too rough. I kept playing with her clit with my finger, flicking it and flicking it. She was going great. The clit was getting bigger and bigger, but then my arms started getting tired. She would just not come or not let me know that she was coming. I could see her balling and moaning, but I couldn't recognize that she came or was about to come. If she did, she would have come hard as fuck from what I was seeing in her reactions, but I didn't know when it was coming or if it came. I just gave up, laid next to her, and went to sleep.

I felt something get up from next to me, but I didn't know what time it was. I woke up, and she was downstairs already and was fully dressed. She said she had eaten already. I went upstairs to take a shower. She went up. When I got out, I wanted to have sex with her again. I felt funny about what had happened the previous night. She didn't say anything as I pulled her closer to me, but she didn't want to go fully. She had to get back on her way to our home city two and a half hours away. I guess she and Hank had both come down for a quickie. She had to go pick him up the girl's place that he had been dealing with. I felt funny after she left.

I felt I could have been a little more compassionate about her being here and not making her wait while I smoked with the fellas. We should have gotten right to it and then all my concentration and lust would have been on spending time with her. I felt I could have done much better and more. I was pissed about my performance I started to trip and think that when she got up in the middle of the night, that she and Lavar did something to help her get more satisfied. Lavar was funny and cool sometimes but a snake-ass nigga on other occasions, so I didn't doubt it if they did do something.

Apartment living with a roommate was cool and all, but if I wanted to creep and do my own thing and not have to worry about others in my business, it was time to get a better living arrangement. I was willing to live with my current roommate but in a bigger and more spacious in the living arrangement. During the last week of the summer program working with the youth on campus, I asked him what the plan for a place was. I asked him if he had been looking. He said in front of everyone that were basically friends with both of us that he didn't want to be my roommate anymore. I was upset when he said that. He had said it in such a sarcastic way as if to say I was no good to be living with or something. A tear started to come to my eye as I said okay. I didn't let it fall out of my eye though. I don't know if anyone noticed it or not, but I did excuse myself. I felt my hand shaking a little bit, but it wasn't moving. I don't know if I was supposed to hit him for messing with me and my mother's credit or if I was supposed to applaud him and celebrate.

Then I thought maybe it was that I robbed some people for money a couple of weeks prior off campus and that maybe he heard about it. Maybe they thought I was hot. The thought of my mother's credit and me maybe not finding an apartment because of an eviction due to him not paying his portion of the rent wasn't concerning me. It was *What if they found out that I robbed some people?* I didn't give a fuck about that nigga. I really didn't care to live with him. I just knew it might have been best to stick with someone you already knew in living together. I knew that it would be hard to find a place unless I paid things up front or a double deposit, which I had no problem doing, but it would have made things harder to do as far as keeping money and paying utilities on time. It could have been achieved though. I think the hurt and illusion or feeling of my hand shaking was telling me to do something to him for trying to play me and put me in that type of situation. Waiting to tell a motherfucker at the last minute, knowing what his initial plans were, the audacity of the fake New York nigga leaving my mom to cover the back rent and shit. I should have smacked him in his fucking face and pissed on him for that for real.

I didn't think that they had known for real because I wasn't in jail, and there were no police questioning me. I did bust a freestyle of the incident beforehand, and I was going to tell the police if questioned that someone might have heard me rapping about it, but I would never do something like that. I guess I never got caught because I didn't bust my gun. I just ran up on the victims and let out a loud scream, like "Roar!" and told them to drop down. They did and I waved the gun at them to go ahead as I picked the money. Just like the freestyle I had busted. I don't know if someone else did a similar robbery or crime or because there were a lot of robberies and crimes that summer; it was hella hot that summer. I heard that my freestyle did make some people want to go out there and commit crimes, but I didn't know who heard me. Really, I was just busting flows. I used to walk and just bust freestyles and others used to listen.

I waited behind the steps in an apartment building off campus. I had my black mask and hoodie on. I just waited. I remember telling myself, *I'm not waiting down here for too long!* I heard the main door open. A White man and a White woman, maybe his girlfriend, walked past. I saw them walk past, and I pointed my gun at them. They started to run down the hallway. I just yelled a loud growl, as loud and as long as I could, pointing the gun at them. I followed them down the hallway, growling the loud yell, and told them to drop down. I said, "Drop down! Drop down!" They stopped at the other door going to the street, and the man threw the money on the ground. I told them to get the fuck out of there by waving my gun to them.

I grabbed the money and went back through the way they came in on the alley part of the building. I started walking fast to not attract attention, like someone actually running from a crime scene. I took the mask off and the hoodie in the process of fast walking. I stuffed the hoodie, mask, and gun into a tight bundle and stuffed it under my white T-shirt with a Cleveland Indians logo on the front. I had worn that shirt to Freaknik that year the first day while down there. It was white, but the Big Chief Wahoo logo on it hid the darkness off the hoodie and things. It just looked like I had a bigger stomach than what I already had. The police might have been responding to the call of someone getting robbed or maybe another call or maybe cruising. They just rode right past me. I just kept walking. At that time, I was almost free of the area, and I was walking regularly. They never stopped me or asked me anything, so I thought I was in the clear.

I guess I was thinking too much about why my old roommate wanted new living arrangements. I then thought of the time at Freaknik when I had taken the rental car and had gotten lost. I didn't mean to get lost; I just did. I kept trying to go back to the hotel, but I kept coming across the same signs of going to detour. Over and over again, like three to four times, I kept seeing the sign to go to a detour. I knew they would have been pissed when I got back so late. I didn't want or mean to go back late. I just wanted to get my kicking it set and done with. They already stated that they were waiting for some more of their friends to go before they got ready to go out. I left them some weed to smoke, about an ounce, that I had traveled with and some spending money. We already paid for the hotel and rental. I was told really fast by Lavar that we were meeting some people, but I didn't know who he was talking about; he said it so quickly like to hide who the person or group was but was saying to praise them like they were something important or something. I was more concerned about getting everything paid for equally.

Freaknik 1993

I did get a chance to kick it after an embarrassing introduction to the guys that we were meeting up with at the hotel. I didn't know any of the guys that Lavar said had the discount on the hotel room. He told me their names like I had known them or I was supposed to. When we got there, it was still dark in the early morning. I said a freestyle with the window down to welcome the city to me. That freestyle was unique. I drove most of the way, mostly through the construction. Edward and his roommate, another one of Lavar's friend, Joe, was in the back seat. Edward was like, "He skilled at it!" as I was speeding through the cones and the construction. We made it safe and saved a lot of time.

We arrived at the hotel but wasn't able to get in right away, so we rode and waited till daylight to get out and see things on foot. We went to a couple of malls. There were girls everywhere. There was so many Black people there; it was incredible. I brought an ounce for us to smoke, but I just knew that there would be more weed. We got something to eat at Burger King, and one of the guys that came with my roommate friend, Greg, who was living from Florida at the time, had a gun with him. He must have been drunk or something. He pulled it out inside of Burger King. We were all like, "Woah! What the fuck is wrong with this nigga." He was cappin', talking about he would bust a cap in whoever and all that strong talk like he was a killer. We all thought he was out of place. None of us wanted to be around him for that entire trip. We, or at least I, came to have a positive experience that motherfuckers wasn't on that level, trying to cause problems or be a disturbance to the city or the event. We walked around a little bit through the city and went to a park that a show was going on at. I saw my sister there with her sorority sisters.

We spoke briefly. I saw some older guys I grew up with under from the hood there too. Everything was good. I had on a Cleveland Indians shirt with the Chief Wahoo logo on it. I came across plenty of people. Some were from Cleveland and spoke about me, saying, "You can tell he from Cleveland!" It felt good to have people notice me with all the different types of Black people there. I started dancing, grooving on a main street we were walking on. A girl pulled up, got out the car, and started shaking her ass in front of me. I grabbed her waist and was pumping her like we were fucking doggy style, and then I slapped her ass. The girl almost fell forward to the ground. She grabbed her head, pulled her hair back, and got back in the car. Everyone was tripping, laughing, and having fun. I had a blunt behind my ear and was advised by Greg that I should keep it on the low. I was thinking, *This is Freaknik, we can kick it. We got the whole city*, but then I saw the police patrolling and put it away.

We got in the room, and everyone was talking about going later on and linking with other people from our college and having fun. I wanted to go ahead and do me right quick and ride to see the city. I wasn't trying to be around, kicking it with the same people from my school. I called my homeboy Hank I grew up with, who would come down to visit me at school and go to the parties. He told me that some of the homies from the hood were down here too. He said that him and some other hood homies were trying to come but wasn't sure if they were or not. I decided to go driving and see a thing in the rental that we all paid for. I told them that I would be right back and left the weed for them to get right with.

I met a girl, and we started talking, exchanging where we were from and things like that. She offered herself to me for $20. She sucked my dick like a pro and I had my finger all in her pussy and ass. We got really nasty in the car. Afterward, I got lost on my way back to the hotel. I started to worry, hoping the guys wouldn't be mad, but it switched to "*Damn, where the fuck am I?*" and I was more concerned about making it back to the hotel safe. I guess my crazy paranoia started to kick in because I started to see cartoons again. I saw Lavar riding next to me, hanging out in the car as I went through the city part of the town and off the freeway. He was mean mugging and started to yell something at me. I didn't know if it was him or not 'cause of the nature of the illusion or whatever it was. I just ignored it and kept driving. As I got closer to the hotel, the city looked better and free from the cartoonish visions, and everything was more peaceful and welcoming. I made it back to the hotel safely.

I arrived at the hotel and pulled in the parking garage. I headed upstairs. I didn't want to explain things right away unless I had to. I was so tired and drained from getting head in the car and driving in circles, trying to make it back. I knew that they would be upset. I said I was just going to throw the keys on the table and say I got lost and explain the rest after I got some rest. I was tired as hell, and I felt like woozy from what I had been through. I went up to the room but wasn't sure exactly what room it was. I knew the corner of the hotel it was in but didn't know the exact floor. I knocked on the door of one room, and it was the room of the guy who had pulled his gun out in Burger King. I looked past him into the room and saw he had his bed ready for company. I said, "My fault," and went to the room one floor up instead. He told me what room everyone else was in.

I got to the room and threw the rental car keys on the table and said I got lost. All I saw was a white flash of light and felt a slight tap on my jaw. I was headed to the bed to collapse anyway. It was like someone had thrown something in my face and tried to sneak me with a hit across the jaw or on the wide of the head. I was moving toward the bed to pass out, so I have a strong belief that whoever it was didn't get the hit like they wanted to. I felt the hit slightly on my chin, but I couldn't see anything, just a white light.

When I woke up on the bed, I was waking slowly, and I saw someone cover my backside up to not show my buttocks. I had always had my pants sagging, so I didn't think nothing of it because I looked back and saw some girls in the room who I had never met before. I thought whoever it was, they were looking out for me to not be ridiculed for sleeping with half my ass showing. I jumped up and went straight to my things to get some clothes out to take a shower. Someone else was in there at the moment. I didn't show any emotion or answer any question to what happened and why I came back so late. When it was my turn to shower and dress, I saw a young guy named Larry, who used to come by the apartment, go past the bathroom door.

He used to come by the apartment and dick ride by showing too much respect to everyone in the apartment in my opinion. He got mad one time and thought I was too wild because I let another guy who everyone thought was wild use my gun once. When I had gave him the gun, we were all out in public on campus, and he had bust off a couple of shots in the air. I used to look out for the little nigga Larry because he ran with some other younger guys that were from my neighborhood. I never had trouble with anyone on campus. I was always strapped. One time, a fraternity member had asked me if he could fight one of the younger homies without me interfering. Larry was pumped when he walked past the room; I thought he was goofy, but it was Freaknik, and the thought didn't go on any further about him.

While in the bathroom, I looked in the mirror, and all I could feel was razors and heat coming from my penis. It was like the mirror was breaking right in front of me, and I was feeling the pain from it on my penis shaft. I felt down below when I sat on the toilet to take a shit. I felt scratches and cut-like marks on my penis shaft. It wasn't bleeding, but it was stinging. I used the toilet, and I didn't have any complications using it, so the wonder of what had happened and waking up to someone covering my backside up wasn't an issue. I flushed the toilet, took a shower, and brushed my teeth.

After the shower, I didn't feel the stinging on my penis. The hot water didn't bother my penis either, but I started to think that maybe my backside was being covered up because someone had just wiped me or something. I didn't think about it further until I saw Greg on the other side of the hotel room, holding his arms up like he was the king of the city or some shit. I felt like this city was too big for a nigga—"You ain't shit, and if y'all did something foul to me, it will come out and be dealt with either by mine or God." I finished getting dressed, and we left the hotel, got in the car in the parking garage, and met some other guys from my school on the side street of the hotel. We only planned to be in town for one to two days. Some had stayed longer, but the guys that I came with in the rental were only staying for one to two days.

We started to head out of the city. No one asked me what happened until we got close to the Chattanooga, Tennessee, freeway signs. I told them I got lost, but I didn't tell them I had gotten some head and my fingers was all in the girl's pussy and ass. I would have if they asked why the car smelled, but they didn't. When I told them in the car that I got lost and that I kept seeing the same signs over and over, trying to get back to the room, Joe—who was with me in the back seat—lowered his head at the same time as if to laugh or maybe he was embarrassed. I forgot about the razor penis and covering me and all by then. I was just glad to be heading back home. Some girls in a car rode past and took the Chattanooga route. They must have just come from Freaknik too. They were still having fun and waving their hands out the window, having a good time. No one said anything about Freaknik or judged me in my face about going back late. No one said anything about jumping me or trying to jump me to show me a lesson for taking the car. No one mentioned anything about the girls in the room and definitely didn't mention anything about the strong cuts and scratches on my penis. I didn't mention it either, but I knew they were shit anyways. I knew that they were upset that I took the car and was holding a secret of what really happened in the room. I had had glimpses of information of what happened when I was waking up. I didn't mention it, and they didn't mention it being sneaky, but I knew that things would come out later. I just wanted to keep being successful and stay focused, so when they spoke, their words would fall off me and I could brandish their ass with shame and hate. Right now, though, I was just glad to be going back to the house and not in the hospital.

We made it back safe, and some of the other guys came back in the rental they had used a day later. The homey from LA had a video of the events at Freaknik. I saw the video of me freestyling and some other footage that I remember, but then I saw a different footage. I saw that someone who had looked like me was at different restaurants and had his head down like he was praying, being silent at each one. It looked like me, but the character was in all blue, and he had a blue aura about him. It was like he was a cartoon. I thought it was an illusion or something, then I thought it was Leonard because they said we looked alike because we were both strong and big in size. I didn't tell or ask any of us watching what I was seeing. I thought it was a special effect or something. I had been so sane and functioning that I had forgotten about all the illusions and hallucinations that I used to have. I didn't say anything because it came across to me that maybe I had missed an entire day at Freaknik. But we had only planned to be there for two days. I recounted the days, and everything added up. I just let the video play, and there was more information on it about the trip and the fun the other guys had. They had a ball, and I was relieved. I was glad they had a good time. Seeing all the girls in the video showing their titties and getting bout was fun to see too. I was glad that they enjoyed themselves.

I got my own apartment after staying at Leonard's and his roommate's place. His roommate named Stag, which was his nickname, was a deejay for some of the campus parties. I stayed with them for just a little bit after the work program with the youth on campus was over. I used to call my parents every once in a while, but then I stopped. They came looking for me on their way back from visiting family down South. They found me when I was walking with my LA homey to turn in his financial aid papers at the register's office on campus. My parents rolled up on us like they had been riding low in deep coat from the way they had pulled up.

My father cursed at me, telling me to get my ass in the car. My LA homey was shocked from the way they had pulled up and said he'd see me later and kept stepping to the campus office. I jumped in the back seat, and they gave me some money to get by while I was staying with my homies. I bought us something to eat when we all got back to the place together. I was waiting to get my financial aid check to pay for classes. I would have at least $1,500 to $2,000 after paying for classes and books. I was looking for a place, but I didn't care where it was as long as I got it.

Chapter 8

New Beginnings at My First Solo Apartment in My School City

I got a place off campus but was a walking distance to the campus. It was located three to four streets over from the last apartment I had with my New Yorker roommate. It was also three streets up from the main street before the campus started. One side of the apartment was the street, and the back side was the alley with parking right under my window. I was on the top third floor. I had used a fake cosigner like my previous roommate did on the lease with me, but I had all intentions of paying my rent and paying on time. I filled the apartment with furniture and music equipment and a twenty-seven-inch box TV. I had cable and a home phone with caller ID. I wasn't worried about paying bills because I had a new work-study job. I was no longer doing receptionist work, where I had opportunities to get unofficial copies of transcripts and tried to get credit cards in other students' names and used the cash withdrawal options once they were sent to abandon houses, which never worked by the way. No, I had a different life, now. A different way of scamming and it was bringing in more money.

I got in the apartment, and I was renting cars to go home for holidays on or just to slide home and see different things. I was with a team I ran with while at work. We all did the same thing. We would meet up, count money, and split it amongst each other. Most times, we were solo, but we all knew what we were doing. Some made $300 a shift. Some, like myself, balanced the shifts. I would get $200 from one shift and $120 from another. Then there were others who stayed in school just to work the job and paid for their house with it. I averaged $4,000 per month after taxes with everything coming in. The girl Lisa who I saw walking with her friend while he was on his bike was now a girl that I was talking to. We would go out, eat, and talk on the phone on occasion. I also met a girl while I was at Freaknik.

I think I went down to the lobby and met her, but I didn't remember going to the lobby. I remember her name and the first digits of her number, but going down to the lobby was blurry and unclear for me to picture or remember. I also thought I had seen Hank and some other friends from the hood in the lobby. They tried to talk to her too, which I thought they were cockblocking. She gave me her number. I remembered her name and the entire conversation. I remember asking my hood homies to go on up to the room, but they said that they didn't want to go up there. As I think about it more and more, I don't know if that event even happened because I had left it all in the past and was just focusing on the present. Whatever they had planned I hoped would fail, and I was still going to be me in all possible ways and deal with them the best way for me, even if it wasn't positive, but I was more interested in just fading them and getting bread.

When I called the girl from the lobby, I found out that she was from the same city where I was in school at, and she was a student at the same school. She didn't ask too strongly of how I got her number. I just told her Freaknik, and the questioning had stopped. We linked up a couple of times. Once to go to a play for one of her classes and another time at my place. While leaving the play, we stopped at a local park while a city celebration event was going on. She told me that she could go anywhere in the city and not get touched, but I couldn't. I felt funny and wanted to say that "I already robbed one of y'all motherfuckers already," but I didn't say a thing.

I think she felt funny because at the play, I had my arm around her like we were together. I felt that she felt uncomfortable, but I wasn't sure if it was that she didn't want my arm around her or if it was just uncomfortable because we were new to each other. She eventually told me that she was going to the military. I later saw her on campus when I was walking with another girl. She looked at me funny, but we spoke. I guess the military was just a front. I guess everything with her was just a front because I never could understand how I met her from being asleep on a hotel bed and waking up with my penis slashed and all. I never had her number in my pocket but knew part of it and her full name. That wasn't the only weird thing I noticed and experienced at that apartment.

I was still smoking weed heavily. I had money coming in, even though it wasn't dope boy money. I really didn't want too much. The best weed came from the White boys in the city and those who were connected with the campus. I would get an ounce like every three days to a week. It depended on the classes and seriousness in timing for midterms and finals. My friends—who I only considered associates now since I had new living arrangements—would come by, smoke, and play video games. I would go over to their place to do the same things from time to time. I had a video game called 360 Pro. It had the best graphics at the time. We would meet at my house and play football and smoke for hours at a time. Niggas couldn't fuck with me on the video games, especially sports, which was all I played. The first time I played the 360 Pro Madden Football Game at another person's house, I was doing all kinds of stuff on the game. I whitewashed the nigga I was playing against. I left him with a goose egg for a score. They were all mad and shit.

We all got back close again like there weren't any issues to discuss. My friend Huko from Africa, whose apartment was entered by the police because of my jerkish hood homey Sylvester, started coming back around. We would play for hours, just him and I. I had respect and love for him. I didn't think he was about any foolishness and had my back when I needed him to, but I rarely did. I never wanted to put him in any foul situation. I never wanted to put any of my friends, associates, or person I dealt with in any type of foul situations. I always agreed to what Brotha Lynch Hung said when he rapped, and he said he had his own back fade. I didn't have a car, and he would assist me in certain things. We would talk about everything, from women to future goals to our associates that we were online with a couple of years back and them secretly joining Masonry without letting us know.

They joined Masonry and didn't let us know as if we were not to be invited by them for some reason. We understood that it is secrecy but the plan to join wasn't. We did everything else together; why not continue from a failed joining of the fraternity we all had tried? He had issues with Greg when he moved back to the school city and joined the brotherhood, and I guess they had issues with me from Freaknik that still stemmed to me seeing them as being wrong more than they saw me, but I didn't consciously know every single detail of the events that fully took place. It was something that Huko and I discussed often, but it was just between us.

I used to get high every day. There was not a day that passed that I did not. One time while chillin' with Huko, about to play the video game, I took a bong hit of some weed called evergreen. It smelled strong like pine cones. I got it from some new White boys I met on campus. I lit the bong and sucked up half the smoke and pulled the stem out of the plug, and it was like heaven came over me. All I could smell was a green forest. My eyes were fixed and wide open, but I was looking through nothing but smoke. I looked to the right, out of the corner of my eyes, while coming back to a regular consciousness, and I saw a cartoon of my friend from Africa who I envisioned doing an African dance or something. I thought it was funny as shit. Man, I was high as fuck off that first bong hit from the evergreen. It was the best I had in college. I had skunk before with my associates, but this weed took me there for real.

My friend and I got so high that night. I felt a new way of being with him. A new way of recognizing what good things in life were. I had a place filled with nice things, a fridge full of food, good smoke, and income coming in, plus I was in school trying to get my GPA up that had recently dropped from trying to join a fraternity. At that moment, I increased on my not-giving-a-fuck attitude about what had previously happened in my life. All the shortcomings that really didn't amount to too much damage in my life, I was willing to laugh at and keep stepping to succeed with no care, no gives, and no regrets.

My homies from the hood still came down to visit. Even my jerkish homeboy. He came down with one of his friends. I let them stay while I was at work. First my homey from the hood had left the nigga with me in my house like I knew the motherfucker! I didn't know that nigga, and Sylvester just left and didn't say nothing. When I went to work the next day, I let him have the key. They were supposed to come pick me up from work. They were two hours late. When they picked me up, I saw they had some of my tapes scattered all in the back seat and cases opened from the hedge. I said something to him about it, and he just looked at his partner in the front. I got out of the house, and I was the first out of the car and the first at my building. I went upstairs to the apartment and didn't let them in. The nigga Sylvester was yelling at me through the door, "That's why niggas in the hood don't fuck wit you!" I wanted to say something back to him, but I just kept quiet, sitting there, waiting for the nigga to leave in front of my door and pull off, not remembering to give my key back.

Another time, two of my homeboys came down. It was unusual because they were just sliding through. One came down previously with Hank. He only came with him, so it was funny that he came with another friend from the hood, who I haven't seen in years. He came before a couple of times. Last time he and Hank came, they came down on switches on the long Cadillac.

His name was Tom—a young dope boy from my hood. We used to lift weights in my parents' basement, and we used to kick it pretty strong. My favorite memory of him was one time during Halloween, he threw an egg from across the street that landed perfectly in a nigga's ear that the hood was tripping on. That shit was funny. He was funny at times to me; we all had good times back in the hood. He came this time in the 'Lac again, and my old-school homey who I really didn't kick it with too much after we did the battle raps and breakdancing way back in the day; his name was Fraizer, but we called him Fraize for short. They wanted to go to a club. I really didn't do clubs in the city and had stopped going to the Icebreakers and other parties. There wasn't any room in the 'Lac for me and the battery charger in the back seat.

My ex-roommate homey Edward wanted to go and offered to drive me, so we all could go. We were split up while heading to the city bar. Last we saw them, a whole bunch of girls were running behind them in a parking lot as they were hitting switches in the 'Lac. I got back to the apartment and waited for them to show back up or call. I was in there, waiting and smoking and smoking and waiting. When they arrived, I thought they were upset, but once I told them that we got separated, everything was good. Tom went in the bedroom and laid on my bed, and Fraize stayed in the living room. We were smoking and watching TV. I went to my bed to go to sleep. I saw Tom was on one side of the bed. I laid on the side that was closest to the wall and away from the door and closet.

When I laid down and turned my head away from everything, I looked up, and again, I saw someone come in the bedroom door. I didn't know what or who it was; it looked like two people rushing in side by side. I was so high that I just wanted to make sure my homey Tom was straight, so I put my hand, hovering over him, as to tell the intruders to not do anything to him. Then instantly before I could attempt to say anything or react to them running in the room, I heard Tom say, "What is this!" I felt myself being pulled on by my legs and felt a thump on my head, but I was so high I couldn't react quick and clear enough to be combative and fell back to sleep. When I started to wake up, I saw someone who had a blurry look of Fraize with their penises in front of my face. I turned my head away. I didn't feel any penis or dick meat in my mouth. I woke up to me turning my head in disgust and anger, but I was still too high or maybe woozy from being hit on the head to be fully combative.

I don't know if my subconscious had been manipulated and was saving me from seeing if I had been sucking some nigga's dick or whatever else. In later years, I learned more about subconscious and its effects and how to become one with it by breathing and meditation. I knew of it at that time and other mental manipulations from watching propaganda and reading, hearing, and learning about it. Since I didn't taste anything in my mouth, I didn't think anything foul had happened to me sexually, but I did wake up with my back feeling funny and my legs feeling like they needed to be stretched out. I didn't think I did anything or that anything of sexual nature had been done to me physically. I got up and went to the restroom, and I had no problem using it, so I just wanted to know more about what all the bullshit was about. The act that was done, as far as the setup, had outweighed the penis in my front of my face. I started to see color again.

Why was it so hard to see exactly who came in the room? I could see them, but it was so glossy it was funny. This was the second time I have seen color of fuzzy illusions since in my dorm room, when I was being hexed or whatever the information that had me jerking and bouncing on my bed when *mi vida* and Crips came to my room and were in the hallway. I was bouncing and jerking in the bed, and all I heard was I was being made a Crip and that I wouldn't be active or claiming strong till later on in life, but that I would click right into it. My room and hallway had so many visitors and different types of people I came across, met, and connected with even if only for a short time.

This time while shitting on the toilet, I wanted answers. I said, "I'm going to let them tell me before I get irate and start demanding answers." When I went into the living room and sat at the connected dining room table, I went straight to the bong to smoke. Fraizer sat across from that at the table. He told me a story as I was starting to light the bong. I offered the bong to him but then pulled it back, so he could finish his story. He told me that his brother and some other family members had stolen from him before and that life is fucked up for everybody. He then started to talk of how hard it was back home and that the hood couldn't trust anybody and repeated about that his own beloved brother was stealing his stash from him. I guess that was the bitch apology he had for me. I ain't even want to hear the shit no more and kept smoking and left him the embers to light up. I was embarrassed to know those niggas at that point. I walked back to the bedroom, and Tom had a funny smirk on his face and started holding his arms over his head like he was holding up the doorway. All I could think was this MF was trying to hex me or asking that this should never leave this room. Either way, I thought they were a bunch of hateful faggot goofballs. All that money in the hood and you on bullshit with me a nigga from the same hood, trying to make good.

I had plans for the hood. My major was criminal justice. I was trying to get a job in helping them legally or be in a position to help them. I had friends on campus I was dealing with outside the Freaknik circle who were willing to specialize in cleaning their money and others who were willing to help them in legal situations as far as lawyers and other positions that were all being set up to help niggas from the hood, and I included them in because I had love for blackness and my niggas. It had been a while since I had been home and wanted to help them achieve greater things, but they fucked me over so fuck 'em. I let those ties to those helping persons go far away enough but close enough for my benefit only.

They then left and I didn't check the safe the next day. I thought one of my student aid checks was missing. I had one in there, but I thought I had two. I thought I had my student loan over payment check and my grant over payment check. I couldn't remember if I had cashed one or not. I got stuck while I was kneeling, checking the safe area that had a key to it. I guess my jerkish homeboy made a copy of the key when he had my keys during all the time when he and his homeboys went to visit. That bitch motherfucker. I knew I shouldn't have let him hold the keys while I was at work. I shouldn't even had let the MF in. I didn't say anything to anyone about my check possibly being missing, except to my ex-roommate at his apartment and later to Huko.

Chapter 9

Middle Time Period of First Solo Apartment and Relations

That apartment was off the chain. There were so many incidents with prostitutes, incidents with my pullback antisocial protective behavior, and incidents of foul play done or tried toward me. I was ashamed to be living in that motherfucker.

I started to spend more time with Lisa, the girl I saw walking that day with the guy with the bike at the last apartment. We would go out to eat and to the movies. We started being more sexual each time she would come and visit. It started when she came over and I kissed her on the cheek while we were sitting on the couch. She blushed, and I felt good because she didn't trip about it. I always had a funny feeling, but with all the nonsense I had been through, I was desensitized to a lot of things and thought, well, maybe she could ride her objective and we could come to a peaceful meeting point.

I had been with prostitutes or boppers came by and gave me sex for money. Some were older and tried to teach me how to fuck at first until I got inside and into stroking them more. Most of them tried to come back over or keep in contact. One girl I was fucking had put her foot in my face while I was fucking her in the missionary position. I never experienced no shit like that before. She was cold in her looks, though. She had long curly hair, a beautiful body, and was light-skinned, which was in at the time. She wanted me to stick it in while she was bent over, looking in the fridge and asking me to make her a steak. I was like, *Hell nawl!* in my head. I grabbed her by the ass and escorted her to the back bedroom. I started stroking inside her. She seemed like she was bothered more than receiving pleasure. It was like she needed a fix of some drugs and wasn't used to having sex without it. I could just notice it from dealing with these type of women in the past.

She wasn't complaining or nothing like that, but I could tell she felt funny. I pushed her legs up to go deeper in the pussy, and one of her feet slapped me in the face. She apologized but only two to three minutes after I had been stroking her. When I busted a nut and I got up to put the rubber in the toilet, I saw her walk past to the kitchen. I guess she was really hungry. I had two thoughts—one to let her cook and fuck my dishes up and have her give me more sex or just kick her ass out 'cause I didn't want to be doing dishes and watching this bitch all night. I chose the second. I kicked that bitch out. It didn't matter how good she looked; she was acting more like a strong geek type the more she got comfortable. I always wanted a girl around the house or coming by. I just wasn't satisfied with the type of females I was choosing to come by. I mean, I did like tricking because I could stop dealing with the girl, and it would be no major confrontation. I didn't have to be bothered with the relationship questioning and attention needed by females. It was in and out, and I'd be back smoking and playing videos games with a fattened penis.

I started getting more sexual with Lisa later. I would kiss on her and suck her breasts and feel on her. I started eating her pussy. I did that two times without inserting my penis. The second time, I saw her looking at my penis while I was licking her clitoris. I was lying sideways. I wanted to get up and insert it, but I wanted to play with her some more. She asked me to fuck her that night. I did, and she asked me before if she sucked my dick, if we would together now. I told her yeah. I didn't mind; we had already been going out and things. I was glad that I made her ask me to fuck her.

Things had been going good with her as far as a relationship. She told me she was blessed while we lay in the bed after sex once. I thought she was on some shit for real then. I thought she was about to do some voodoo crazy chick head shit to a nigga or that she was going have her people get me in all kinds of bullshit if I did her wrong. I didn't plan to do her wrong, so I wasn't stunting what she was saying but stayed, knowing more strongly from her statement. I met her parents and even came by once or twice. She stayed in the same state as me but in a different city from where our school was located. I liked how she would say she wanted to suck my dick and would get impressed by the sizes that she could make it to.

I used to have dinner parties, and she attended one with me. They were at my place, and my friends would come over. My ex-roommate friend Greg said that "She adores you!" Things were funny, though; I didn't fully trust the company I was around most times except for Huko. It seemed like I didn't like too many people interested in what Lisa and I had going on after Greg told me that at the dinner party. They all left. I started cleaning up the kitchen, and then I grabbed her to the counter of the kitchen that separated the kitchen from the dining room. I started kissing her, lifted her up, and placed her on the island countertop. I started to eat her pussy, and then we went to bed for the night. Lisa was cool but didn't like me smoking too much. She never said it but mentioned how much I was smoking and when I wasn't. I usually wouldn't smoke as much with her around as I did with the fellas. Her pussy was clean, and she seemed to be more down for me than against me, but things change when other people are interested in your relations.

I was told by a female friend that I used to visit the ones who work at the front desk dorm. That people were going to get jealous because of me being in a relationship and to watch out for certain females. I had a bunch of female friends, but we were just friends. I never had sex with them but jokingly gave compliments and suggestions of sex. Some smoked weed and others didn't. Some came by just to see how I was doing or pick up a mixtape. Others I considered my sisters, and we just kept each other in good spirits. They knew I was dealing with Lisa, or they at least knew I had someone I was dealing with. I never included Lisa's and my business to them, except for hope she was my closest play sister down there. It wasn't anything negative, but there was always good advice and conversation.

One female friend had come by to smoke with me and the fellas. I flirted with her in the past, but we were just cool. We all got high, and I went to lay down. I left my company in the living room because my homeboy Gevis from high school was in town and stayed with me before he had a business venture to attend to. We both laid down, and I was resting on top of her to the side. I felt her side and rubbed back and forth between her hip and her breast. I didn't proceed any further and fell asleep; from then on, I don't know what happened. All I remember is a finger reaching toward my buttocks and someone pricking me in my ass.

I also remember seeing the hand in an illusion or unusual way. It was like I was looking at it being done from the back of my head. I saw her get up and go into the next room. I recognized other things going on in the room as well. I heard someone sucking dick or at least the lip smacking and slurping sounds. I could remember the thought of or at least it seemed as though they were trying to make a very disrespectful impression upon my head. Again, I wasn't combative, I couldn't wake up fully and respond physically. I thought that girls would put a finger in a man's ass when she thought he was a fag or couldn't get it up. The only reason I didn't try to have sex with the girl was because I didn't want the guys in the other room to come in and expect anything. I didn't want to get in trouble or see things as a setup for her or me.

Anything else that happened that night, I didn't give a fuck about. I dropped her off the next morning in my friend from high school's car. It was like nothing happened at all. The next week, she came over to smoke again, and my girl came over and wanted to ask who she was. My friend said to me, "I know you ain't been telling my business!" I don't know why she said that because we had no business.

My girlfriend and I had good times and li'l arguments or misunderstandings at the time, but everything was good. They were mainly just discussions about what she had heard, but they were really what she was feeling. Once she told me her friend that she used to fuck back home said that I definitely had someone in my home city. I guess he was still trying to fuck if he wasn't already. One time, she asked me for a pair of shoes. I said that I would buy them, but I was taking care of getting a car and wouldn't be able to right away. I was already getting her hair and nails done. We were already going out and eating, and we really didn't hurt for nothing, but I wanted to focus on stacking money for a car of my own. She got fat while I lost weight while fucking her. I used to work out too. I told her I was trying to be a good man to her and keep myself up. She helped me get in shape because I lost weight by fucking her pussy every time she came over.

Once while she was getting dressed, I noticed that she had a new pair of shoes. This was after she came back from a party smelling like cigars. I thought her girls put her up with coming over with that smell on her breath because of me smoking and possibly smelling like smoke while with her in bed. I thought she and her girls were petty for that shit. I had sex with her that night anyway, and she stared at me smiling while holding my penis after we were done. I didn't feel special by it. In fact, I was actually annoyed by it. Then this li'l shit here with the new shoes. While she was putting them on, she must have noticed me looking at her differently because she stumbled and lifted herself up like she got caught or something and that she needed to explain or it was something that she couldn't explain. I don't know if she bought the shoes or not, if her mother bought them or what. All I could think was that the nigga at home that was she was telling me about was getting in good, and she let him by accepting the shoes, and she probably was back fucking the nigga if she wasn't already. I didn't care at that time. Looking back, I think differently on the decision I made on what to do next, but at that point in time, I didn't care.

One time I had a chance to cheat on her and I did. When the girl was sucking my dick, I felt something go through my penis, but it wasn't come or pre-cum. It was an illusion. It was illustrating to me that I had lost whatever was intended for me or put in place by my girlfriend's sex and future. I did what we did and escorted her out. She came back the next day with one of her girls for a threesome. I left them cursing at me at the door. I didn't invite that bitch back over. I didn't want to start anything with the bitch or her girl no matter how good a threesome sounded. I still wanted to see what was real with Lisa. Our relationship reminded me of my parents' relationship in ways. The aspect of doing the right things the right way as far as being a couple, and sticking with it was starting to sound like a good idea at the time.

I told my girl I had cheated on her. I told her to see if the relationship—which was stagnant to me—would go further and be successful. I wanted her to say that she had cheated on me too, but she never admitted it. I felt that I was just going through the motions of the relationship and really wasn't sure if I wanted to go further, but this would be a great test that would last if our relationship was strong enough. I was willing to be a good super nigga if things would have been good through this test. I was in a relationship, but it was more to please the identity that my parents had and not for me to enjoy.

At least this was what I had in my thoughts. I didn't know which one to make a reality of. We both were about to graduate from school. She was before me, and I needed to get my GPA up. We had been through a lot, even an abortion, but I never honestly believed that the child was mine. I paid for it because I had money coming in good, but I wasn't sure it was mine. We were having unprotected sex, but she had a guy at home putting things in her ear, and she wasn't trusting of me, so I didn't know what to think for real. I paid for it and was supportive in her recovery. She slept and rested at my place for a while after the procedure, and I didn't smoke to bring about any stressful mood.

And then the next couple of days, I told her I didn't I want to see if she would still stick to dealing with me, and she did to a certain point. I could see her nose flaring when I told her I didn't. The next couple of evenings, I remember asking her to marry me. I was standing in the kitchen, and I saw a bright sphere like a constant camera flash to the left side corner from me, behind her, behind the couch. It had to be an illusion. I started to feel like my family in Chicago was watching me. I started envisioning my aunts and cousins from there, and it was like there was an important family thing going on. It was like the spotlight was on me. It was so strong that my shoulder started to feel funny. She said no, and I remembered when I cheated on her with a girl back home, who I had sex with outside in the park when my family from Chicago came to visit.

I felt like she was right, I didn't need or deserve to get married. I never asked her again. We remained together as a couple I guess. One time while having sex on the couch, she said she couldn't hang. My dick was superlong, and I saw her head motion of pleasure when I put it in from the back, and she was on top while I was sitting on the couch. I don't know if she was tired from someone else or not, but it was cool.

That apartment was full of adventures and all types of things. I would be asleep or trying to go to sleep and hear questions if I would help the people in Cleveland. I said no because of the way I was asked. I was trying to sleep. I would hear someone in the hallway by the door just about every night. I didn't check every time; actually, I didn't check at all.

As long as they were not trying to come in, I was cool. I had my gun and slept with it, along with my chain and medallion that hung from it. The medallion was important to me because it was of Mother Mary with a bright halo. It was also special to me because it was real gold and couldn't be duplicated. I've never seen another like it. I got it from my ex-roommate Lavar's cousin. I only paid $250 for it, but it was real gold from jump, but I let my girlfriend and one of my friends, Edward, wear it on separate occasions while they went out. Edward wore it to a club. This was the same original friend of my roommate who took me to court when my roommate and I were about to get evicted.

He used to come over to my place and play video games and smoke. He would tell me things of how my old roommate and his old roommate were, and we understood that both of us were try-ing to get away from the situations we were in. He was being more responsible and had his own place and a lady friend who had moved in and he was dealing with. I knew he wouldn't play me. He was cool and had his own things going on for himself. My girl wore it, but I don't know where she was going with it. She could have let her ex from home wear it or just flaunt with it like, "Yeah, I got this nigga in a fool status." You never know who will do you or what they will do if you lend things out them and are not around to see them with it or using it. I was wearing the chain while sleeping after I had gotten it back from both of them, but it started turning my neck dark, but that medallion was real gold for sure.

The most important thing I was with at night was my trusted gun. I had plenty of guns. I usually had two personals—one bigger handgun and one smaller handgun. I usually had a nine-millimeter, but during my last couple of incidents in that apartment, I had a .45. I would sell guns from time to time. I made a couple of connections doing so too. I was known on campus for having and carrying a gun and smoking weed.

I had purchased a car—a 1989 Chevy Beretta. I had six-by-nine speakers in it, but I had a high-quality tape-and-CD combo player in the dash. My bass was still good to enjoy like the Renault I had in the hood during high school. One time during the morning hours, I heard glass shattering. I jumped up and saw two White boys breaking in my car. I grabbed what I had at that time—a nine-millimeter—and yelled while pointing it out the window, "Get the fuck away from my shit before I blast you!" The White boys looked up, and they looked like birds with their long noses and the look of their wide eyes looking up at the nine. It made me see them as cartoons. They reminded me of the cartoon character Birdman. They flew like Birdman too. I didn't shoot because I knew the law. It cost me gas for the trip to the glass company, the price of the glass, the installment, and time to do all of being mad and calming down. It was too much just for a regular car. I thought it must have been something else, like maybe the White boys were jealous or didn't want me trying to pick up one of their White girls and fuck her.

Another time was when I was asleep, and I thought someone was near me, but I had my gun in bed with me. I said in my head, *If they come through the door, this time, I was gonna get buck and chase them out of the spot, bucking at their ass.* My attitude was "fuck it." It was going to be a struggle. I mean, I slept good at night, but things were happening when I was asleep. I would be comfortable and have some good rest, but things were happening.

One time while sleeping, I woke up to a girl riding my penis. I had sex with someone while I was asleep. I must have had blindfolds on because I felt her on top of me, and I felt my penis being stroked on, but I couldn't see who it was. I hoped it was a girl. She was moaning and trying not to moan too much. I could feel others in the room too. At that time, I had no idea that it could have been a male or a child or whatever. At that time, it felt the resemblance of a female, but there was so much bullshit going on. My mind would wonder on things of identity. I saw and then quickly fell back to sleep. I also had felt my penis being sucked on while I was asleep, but it quickly changed to just smacks of someone's lips as I started wakening more. I thought someone was trying to play with my mind. I tried to get up but couldn't. I quickly fell asleep again but, this time, with a better idea of what the fuck had been going on, but I was still ignorant to it by not being able to get up and turn the lights on or be combative.

This time, I was going to keep it gangster and dangerous. I guess I was a gangster because I was a schoolboy in a city by myself. That is according to what the hood friends who supposedly didn't fuck with me were trying to have me as. I put my new toy—a .45— at the corner of the desk, which was in front of the bedroom window and next to the sliding door closets. I sat on the bed and looked at the closet doors and just listened to what I could hear. I still felt something close to me. I laid back on the bed and stayed up for a while but fell asleep, knowing a little more or at least being able to see it more from the mistake made by hearing smacking lips and what I had been manipulated to see. The next morning, I got up and walked to the desk where the .45 was. I reached for the .45 and heard the sliding doors open and saw a little figure fall out of the closet. The figure of a person fell out of one of my saved big cardboard speaker boxes the system came in. The box fell over, and it was a girl with a black face. She was a small, slim girl. She had tan pants on. I remember because it was the first thing I saw after God talked to me.

While reaching for the gun on the desk as soon as I started to hear the sliding doors, the streetlight outside, which was on in the morning sometimes, had grabbed my face, and all I saw was a smiling face on top of my face. I was stuck for only a moment, but it felt like a couple of minutes. It was like I was being asked to spare the girl. If she was in the closet that entire time, she could have gotten out if I heard her or not and at least gotten her hands on the gun and blasted me while I was asleep. I guess I wasn't gangster but was a fool. I should have checked the entire apartment before I laid down.

The light was strong, but it wasn't hurting me and didn't make me feel uncomfortable. In fact, it was very welcoming and funny that it had a good feeling, a good vibe to it. It was smiling on my face and giving me an impression of look at the silly bitches and please spare them. The light was like when I was younger, I would ride with my father and look into the sun through the windshield while the windows were rolled down. I used to look at the sun and close my eyes; I felt the warmth of the sun and my eyelids would be so soothing. The red, orange, and yellow from the light of the sun was what I had seen with a smiling face and the colors being white and black crayoned in, but it to was light and welcoming.

When I saw her fall, I saw the tan pants and then the face. It was a black face. It looked like the girl used black shoeshine with Vaseline around the edges where her hair would start to come in. She fell out of the box as the box fell over. She got up, then walked extremely fast to the bedroom door. She didn't run, but she was fast with it. When she reached closer to the front door, past the bedroom door, and past the bathroom, I followed her. She opened the door, turned, and started to throw some hand signs up. I couldn't recognize the signs. It was like she was fiddling with her thumbs. I don't think she was able to finish what she was trying to gang sign, then she ran out the door. She was probably too nervous to properly do the correct signs. She flew out the doorway and down the stairs. I didn't chase. I noticed that she was slim with no major ass hips or breast features and had long black hair. I thought later that it might have been a White girl and a sorority prank.

I made sure the door was closed after she ran out. I stared at the door and thought, *Well, goddamn.* I am glad that I didn't shoot that girl if she was doing it for a sorority or a gang or whatever. She still would have been a White female in my house that I had killed or injured. I didn't have licenses for my guns. They were just bought from the gun store, and they could be traced, plus I had receipts thinking I was legal but I actually wasn't. That was the main reason why I wasn't worried about not shooting her. It was racial and not God greatness and love for the human being that made me not shoot her. Yes, I indeed felt the presence of a higher power.

Nevertheless, the way things were happening in that apartment, someone would get something tragically done to them. I believe that God made sure it wasn't me. Just think, a big Black nigga with bad to average grades, smoked marijuana, under further investigation of all kinds of things of bad behavior, and having guns on federal school property would come out. All that wrapped up against a White girl who may or may not have put black shoeshine and Vaseline on her face. I felt afterward that they could have made it out for me being the one who put it on her. I didn't know what the plan on the other side was with what the girl was doing, the other side of school community, and the other side of the police and other authorities.

Their other side mattered. My side of going and sticking to school while working, my side of having my own place and maintaining it like a regular US citizen didn't matter. It definitely didn't matter that I didn't shoot the girl or that I felt the comfortable and a welcoming presence of a higher power with me or that if asked what the presence remind me of, and I say it reminded me of when I used to ride with my father when I was a kid and hearing him say, "You don't have to do it," while looking at the sun and feeling warmth and comfort in my eyes on occasion as a youth. None of that mattered because it was a racial incident. It was a gender issue as well in my opinion. It felt as if I was to shoot her and with her being a female, *White* female, that I would have been the one in trouble because females and White people do not act like that in a regular society. I must have been the perp or the culprit because of my status and behavior of weed-smoking and gun-carrying activities; not just being Black alone but I am the sin of my skin in a regular society.

After escaping jail or prison time by not shooting the black-faced bitch, I felt that I was a killer for real. I felt that God had to step in and save that girl, but in actuality, he was saving me from a bigger downfall. I sat there and thanked God for a while, and it made me wanna laugh, but I didn't want to break the silence of madness that I was experiencing while thanking the Lord for help in possibly saving my life.

It seemed as ever since I had been at school, I was considered a lik of some sort. I know I had things, but I didn't see others actually being jealous of me. I saw them more as being mad because I didn't go through the routes that they took to get a name, to get girls, and get money. I later learned that sometimes others are not jealous of you but jealous of your life. Things that you do to help yourself might hinder someone else's life. It disturbs their thinking and ways. They feel stressed for personal reasons and reasons that are social and can't be explained. The "why him and not me" factor was abundant in my life. It was like I was doing my own thing and starting to be more successful in coming back from incidents that would have made others chalk it up, go home, or stop and change their lifestyle. I didn't and kept motivating myself to do and be better. I had a saying I used to go by and still do to this day: "Who is better, the best, or better? The best will always do fine, but to be better than the best is what I strive for!" One way to keep myself motivated was smoking marijuana.

I was seeing illusions, and my mind was being victimized from time to time. The illusions I saw, I could handle. They made sense and didn't have me in deep thought, wondering what they meant; it didn't invoke in me trying to explain what they meant to myself over and over again. I was on no medication, except for self-medicating marijuana. I had not been diagnosed and never sought help in any fashion. I was getting high and fading the world, as I called it. It was all mind motivation for me to do and be better. The marijuana medication would always correct a corrupt- and hurt-thinking mind. It made things that I was going through more bearable because the high always lifted my spirits about my situation and position in life.

Chapter 10

Trying to Continue Education Career and Everyday Marijuana Use

I would get high off of seven bong rips before I would walk to campus from my apartment. I would have taken three to four while getting dressed, and then the rest after I had gotten dressed. I remember listening to Wu-Tang while walking on campus. My hood homies always thought New York niggas were crazy, and everyone on campus thought my city and suburb city was filled with nothing but scandalous niggas that couldn't be trusted. I was told this by some of the people on campus that came from different areas of the state. My hood homies were now listening to music that they once called "basement music" when I was listening to it in high school. Now that I was listening to more New York and East Coast rappers, I was considered strange by them, but I didn't give a fuck.

While walking on campus, listening to Wu-Tang and Mobb Deep and then switching the sound style to Brotha Lynch Hung, I would watch the White people and others on campus. I used to see how they looked while the music was playing in my headphones. I was high out of my mind every day. While walking, I noticed things of and about the people I was seeing. I knew it could have been illusions, but I didn't care. I was high and having a good time. I was motivated to be better and kept everything positive, even though some of the illusions were not positive. Some of the White people I saw while I was walking seemed to have energy that lunged at me when certain information was heard from the music. Most of the White people, Indian, and Oriental looked broken by the information coming from my music.

I would make it to class sweating, and I could smell the marijuana and bong residue coming off of my clothes and out of my pores from sweating. It didn't matter to me. I was in class, raising my hand and answering questions and being more attentive. I got noticed by a couple of professors and a couple of students who wanted to study with me. I was acing tests, and I was happy I was bringing my GPA back up.

Things started to go bad for some of the younger guys I knew. They were from my old suburb city. They were doing well but had some setbacks, like break-ins and arrests that could have been serious jail time. I bought a quarter pound of weed from one of them. It was garbage weed—black and had no smell to it. I bought it anyways because I knew he needed some extra ends to relocate from his apartment from being broken into while he was asleep with his new child and baby mother. This was the first time I bought bunk weed from a homeboy just to help 'em out. I had money to do so and li'l homie was a good dude, so I didn't mind. My other young homeboy had gotten arrested in another state for some pounds. The police kept him but let him go because they wanted to find the bigger person involved with what he was doing and others that had been supposedly traveling in and out of state with weight.

A guy from the downside of the block of my neighborhood was claiming that he was a snitch and that I shouldn't trust li'l homie. I didn't see any problem in dealing with li'l homie because I wasn't buying any weed from him. He didn't have to know where I was getting my weed from either if he already didn't know it. He came by, and we would talk like old times. I told him I had sex with a girl I knew he liked. I was lying to him just to see how he would react to other questions. I didn't come out and ask him about the arrest and his situation. I wanted him to tell me out of being stressed about the information given to him about a girl he liked. I really didn't like lying on my dick, but it was just a technique, and I didn't think it would truly hurt no one.

It wasn't just the young homies who had a rough time from living in the school city and trying to make things happen without going back home. I let a guy named Herman, Herm for short, I knew from campus who was in a fraternity that used to throw parties at the Union Hall spend the night. I was giving him a ride home to the greater city where I was from. He was an okay kinda dude. I really never had problems with him. He confronted my jerkish friend once before and asked him to fight behind a building, and my jerkish friend refused. I respected him for that, even though I didn't really know him. He came by and I felt something about him. He told me he was big on God. Two weeks earlier, Edward who gave me the ride to court told me that Herm was big on God now and that dude was acting weird. I let him, and when he walked past, I felt funny about him.

We smoked a blunt, and he would start talking about God and things. I talked to him about things I had known. Everything went smooth until he had to use the restroom. I told him, "Let me clean it first." As I was cleaning the toilet, he walked in and praised my last name, saying that we were always good people. I didn't know what the fuck he was talking about. I thought maybe he was being funny like we were toilet cleaners or maybe he was just high and being appreciative.

While I was trying to sleep, I heard Herm smacking and slurping his lips. My penis felt funny, like it was being sucked on. I knew he was in the next room on the couch, and I was in the back in the bed. But those slurps I felt on my penis. I didn't like the feeling, and I thought that maybe the guy was gay or something. The next day, I got up, showered, and got dressed. He took a shower after me, and while he was in there, I felt something come over me. I just started to cry. I don't know why either. I called one of the homegirls from campus, and she said that he wasn't in his right mind at the moment and that I should be careful around him. I don't know why I was crying.

There was no reason for me to be crying. We left, and it was like the guy was just too nice and friendly. He didn't do anything extraordinary or nothing; maybe it was just me. I was driving up the highway toward home, and he would mention how I was driving and my spacing between the cars. It was like he was trying to analyze everything I was doing to figure out more about me. I looked and watched him through my peripherals because I just didn't trust him. All the way home, I had a beam on him. When I dropped him off, I felt relieved. When I got to my parents' home, I started to feel funny again and seemed to be associated with him. The only thing I thought was to kill that motherfucker. I sat on the porch, then I jumped in the car. My mother came on the porch to sit. I sat in the car and contemplated what was going on and what I was going to do. I looked at my mother, and I saw her head drop. I knew then that maybe it was meant for me to do a little time if I got caught. I rode all the way on the other side of town to go kill the motherfucker.

I was tripping because I left my gun at my apartment at school. I wanted to ride clean, smoke-free, and keep safe. I didn't realize that I left the gun until I reached halfway there while on a main street. I saw a car next to me with White boys in it. I saw them say he going up there and even got his gun. It wasn't them actually saying it. The White boys were just smiling because I was bumping music, and they looked my way. I knew they didn't say anything, but I still got pumped and mad from the illusion. I guess I had poor impulse control or maybe I just didn't want to calm down. The urge was uncontrollable, but it wasn't against the White boys.

I knew what I wanted to do. I made it to the community where I had dropped him off at. I rolled around, erratically looking for him, asking questions if anyone had known him. It came to a point that some wouldn't say anything to me and went inside the house. I pulled off with my tires screeching. I felt satisfied for what I did without any gun to show, threaten, or use. My impulse control wasn't my best quality at that point in time. Having a cool head and trying to be understanding wasn't an option that I looked to at that point.

I remember getting my last sack at that apartment for one of the most major incidents in my life that occurred. I came across many situations in that apartment. From friends coming to visit and one of them flipping on my college friends—who at the time I didn't appreciate but later thanked him and apologized that I said something to him about it—to all the females and illusions that I wasn't on meds for. The illusions and hallucinations were all manageable up to a certain point. One time while thinking about home after just hearing a voice while lying down; I didn't know where it came from, but I did notice a cordless house phone under my pillow once. Then the next day, it was gone. I don't know where the other voices came from. Maybe it came from the door or staircase again.

It asked, "Would you help the people in Cleveland?"

I said, "Naw, I'm taking care of myself!"

Later that evening, I walked in the kitchen and saw the devil in my living room. I guess it was the devil? I don't know what else to call it! It was a li'l man, about three to four feet tall, brown skinned with a Cleveland Indians hat on. He looked dirty, and he had an evil grin on his dirty face. He said, "You got it!" while he waved his finger in the air. He started walking from the love seat, which was against the wall at the end of the apartment, and disappeared by the time he made it close to the front door. I was shocked and didn't know what to think. I bought a sack the next day.

Chapter 11

Beginning of Harassing Mental Health Problems and Predetermining Being Labeled a Schizophrenic

I smoked on the new sack I got for two to three days. After that, I started to notice things. No one was at the door that I noticed. They were voices coming from everywhere. They were coming all at once but back-to-back. It was fun at first, but it seemed as the more I had fun, the more aggressive the illusions and hallucination became. It was like they were intentionally trying to break me. The more I wouldn't let them by using wit and not being afraid to answer them and achieve some strength about myself, the nastier and more hateful they became.

I had illusions and experience of me growing out of my mother and father and physically bumping into a figurine. It was one of my neighbors' mom back in the suburb city I was from. It was an illusion, but I physically felt it. The message that I received was that I wasn't going anywhere, that I wasn't grown yet, and I needed to behave. I shook it off, complaining with a loud, "Fuck you!" I stood in the corner of the bedroom by the closet and window facing the room, and I saw illusions of all my family members standing against the wall and all of them approving of me growing out of the family except for one. I couldn't recognize the voice and didn't think he was family. I still don't know who it was supposed to represent.

Even with all the illusions coming back-to-back, I still had my head together to recognize that they were just trips. At the time, I didn't think it was from any foul weed or wrongdoing from anyone. I was just listening, seeing, and answering the illusions. They were more than just voices. The experience had reached to a physical level, and my senses were being enhanced. I was smelling and tasting, seeing and hearing, and also touching and feeling the illusions and hallucinations. It lasted for three to four days. I didn't leave the apartment, and I barely ate during the mental episode.

I didn't know what was going on for real, but I still felt comfortable for some reason. I thought for a moment that my father and grandparents had put a hex on me a couple of weeks before my grandparents on my father side from down South had called. I was high and had been drinking some brown liquor. My grandfather asked me something, and the only thing I could say was murmuring. I don't know what I was saying for real. I knew that I would never disrespected them, but it was funny the way it was slurring out of my mouth. It stopped and the regular voice and conversation continued. I hung up after the conversation later to find out that my father was pissed at me for saying whatever I had said over the phone, and I didn't even know what I said really.

The last night of the episode in that apartment at that time was very disturbing. I had started seeing hieroglyphics. I saw a man riding on skates, crying, and I saw the third eye symbol floating in the air. I jumped up to use the toilet, and when I looked in the mirror, I saw the third eye on my forehead. I looked at it and went back to the bedroom to lay back down. When I laid back down, I saw the sky turn red, and I laid on my side to avoid looking at it. When I did, something came over me extremely fast. It was talking to me with a strong male voice. I started turning in the bed. It was like something had lifted me up and turned me around while I was in the lying position. It turned me as if I was being roasted over an open flame. Then it dropped me and fixed my hands in a position with my one right leg bent to the side slightly but spread apart, my one left arm bent under my pillow, and my one right arm spread out. I felt them being placed like a human was doing it, but there was no one else in the room with me. I got upset, but my penis got hard and stiff.

I turned over on my back and pulled it out to say, "Fuck you," to the red sky. When I did that, it was like a hand came from inside of me and pulled my penis in. It was the hand of one of the hood homies who I had noticed had his penis in my face when I was waking up. My penis was still the same hard and stiff in the fuck-you position, but then I felt and heard a snap like scissors. My penis had been cut! I felt it too much for it not to actually happen. I jumped up and went to the bathroom. I used the bathroom to urinate and felt pain. I had a little dick. It was so small I could barely hold it. I needed tweezers to hold my penis correctly. I don't know what the fuck had happened to it.

I didn't know what was happening to me. I looked in the mirror before going back to lay down, and I saw my face had a green-like mist about it. I just shook my head and laid back down. All those illusions coming back-to-back were incredible and scary because I didn't know what they truly meant. Maybe I wasn't supposed to find out what they meant, and I should have just left the apartment and went to the hospital.

When I laid down, I heard a loud rumbling. It had turned into a voice. It had a message with the voice. Without the voice saying it, I had information and knew it was God. At least it was supposed to be God I was hearing with a strong White-man voice that rumbled and laughed like it was passing by, flying in and out, being heard. I started seeing white flashes of light. I started talking to it, and every time I made sense of what I was saying, it would disappear with a strong rumbling laugh. It would come back with a loud rumble, and I would see the flashes of white light again.

It told me to just be myself and rumbled away with a loud rumbling laugh on the way out. I then heard some feminine and soft voices, saying, "Get him! Get him!" And the sky turned a darker red into a purplish color. I then heard a voice saying that God was dead. I waited and the full regular night came. My penis was still hurting. I tried to pull it out. I kept grabbing and feeling on it. I called my mother and told her I think I needed to come home for a couple of days. I would come home often, but I didn't want to scare her. I wanted to tell her what was going on, but I just couldn't come and say it like it actually was. It was too fresh of an incident to fully explain to myself, let alone to anyone or someone as caring as a mother. I told her I was on my way.

I didn't even grab my toothbrush or nothing; I just grabbed my keys, locked the apartment door, and got in the car with my house shorts and T-shirt on. I pulled off, and when I started to get on the freeway, the trucks that were traveling behind me and passing looked to have devil horns. The red from the front reflectors and the headlights brought about more illusions. I saw the full face of the devil as a bull with red eyes. Every time a truck passed by, the face of the devil would rush toward me. I would look in the driver's side mirror, and I saw a black figure sitting in the back seat. I didn't think it was a person, and it jumped out the window and flew away.

As I kept driving farther, I started to smell manure. As the devil's face would rush toward me when the trucks would pass by, I would feel sensations on my face. The smell and the sensations on my face quickly turned into me smelling and feeling manure being poured on my face. I felt I was being shitted on! It started from the right and went to the left side of my face. I was in the fast left lane, and the illusion had gotten so great that I was almost blinded. The smell and the feeling of shit being poured on me covered damn near my entire face. I could only see from the corner of my left eye.

I was still driving the highway speed limit, but the only thing I could see from the left corner of my eye was the yellow stripe line before you go into the middle railing barriers or median. I almost crashed a couple of times. I tried to keep the steering wheel straight and use the yellow line as a guide to keep driving correctly. I jerked the wheel a couple of times and almost hit the median concrete wall once and another time almost drove into the lowered grass section between the sides of the freeway. I almost died that night. I was tripping the entire two-and-a-half-hour drive.

I made it to the exit for the neighborhood, and things calmed down. When I pulled up to the beginning of the hood, I saw lights flashing on top of some of the late-night people who were outside in the hood. I pulled away from the apartment around 11:30 p.m., and I made it home still driving the speed limit. It must have been close to 2:00 a.m. I went into my parents' house and yelled to my mom that I was home while walking up the stairs. My sister was done with school and was working while living at home to get her own place and things for it. I laid on the bed, and my mother got up and went to the bathroom. I asked what was wrong with me when she went past the bedroom door from the bathroom back to her room. She told me to try and get some sleep and we would find out what was wrong in the morning.

While I lay there, I heard a car pull up in front of the house corner to my parents' house, on the side of the house across the street that faced a numbered street off my street. It was bumping music. Then I heard a voice say, "What you gon' do, the hood or school?" I was at the point where I couldn't tell if it was actually a person saying it or an illusion. I heard the voice and recognized who it was. It was a homie from the hood, that MF Fraizer. I just had an illusion of him in my apartment when I was in my high stupor before things got realer and my penis was hurt. He was hanging in the air, rapping with the New York group Wu-Tang Clan. He started kicking dust on them before the illusion had disappeared.

I dozed off for a moment, and I woke up with the same question—the hood or school—while I felt my shoulders moving, shifting back and forth with the question. Each shoulder represented what was being said. The hood up on one shoulder and the other down or up for school and the other one down. I was shifting back and forth, lying on the bed. The illusions were still strong; the tripping wasn't over. I was once asked by my father if I wanted to work with him at a car factory plant, but I chose school because I was almost about to graduate. I didn't correlate the two at the time. It was more of a jealous hood thing going on in my mind at that time. I left my strap back at the apartment in school. I wonder sometimes what I would have done if I had had it with me. I felt niggas really didn't want me to succeed, and things were just beginning. I got some rest, but I still remember the low bass of the car outside.

My mother had me get up and go with her and my sister. My sister was driving, and my mother was in the front seat. I was in the back, and it was a horrible ride. We went to a couple psych places, and I couldn't talk for myself. It was like a feeling of exhaustion but with a tweak of "if you get up, I'mma get you." I would fight it and be true to my strength of not giving up, and things would calm down for minute. My stomach would stop hurting, and I would stop shivering. But then it would come right back. I heard them talking of admitting me at some places, but I was never admitted into psych service places. While we were driving from facility to facility, I felt my nuts being squeezed so hard that they were hurting an unbearable pain. I cried to whoever was in the front seat, "My nuts! My nuts! My nuts hurt! Something keeps squeezing my nuts!" I saw my sister get on the phone. I don't know if she called someone or if someone had called her. I was out of my mind tripping. The back seat ride was not comfortable at all. I felt like the guy I had beaten in Subway during my freshman year. It was like little birdies were flying over, circling my head. I was awake, but I was out of my mind.

I got to a hospital and was admitted. I remember being rolled to the restroom by a Black female nurse. I was urinating, and my penis was thick and was not affected by being pulled off from the hand that came from inside of me, the scissor noise, and hurt of it being cut illusion. I felt safe for a quick second. Then the nurse opened the door. I guess it was just to check on me, but I heard her say, "Hell yeah! Save some of that good dick!" I didn't see her mouth move, and I saw a bunch of light on her face from the hallway door being opened and the semidarkness color difference of the darker light in the restroom.

I then was in an examination room with my sister and mother. I was just sitting there, and I asked them what had happened. They started to talk to me, but all I heard was "You had died." I then saw a figure, an all-black one, hanging and dangling in front of me. It rushed and jumped into me. I was blinded, and all I could do was scream and say, "I didn't want to die!" My mother or my sister grabbed my arm to try and control me to calm me down. I don't know who it was because I was blinded by the black thing rushing toward and through me. Before it had rushed toward me, it stomped its foot while dangling in the air and shook its head from side to side. It wasn't like the illusion of Fraizer rapping. It was much bigger, like a person right in front of me, but it wasn't touching the ground and came from out of nowhere. After I screamed I didn't want to die, it finished passing though, and the doctor came in. They gave me a shot, and I woke up the next day, I guess, in a hospital room. A nigga in the next bed said I was crazy! That motherfucker didn't even know me. When he said it, he ran his finger across his nose and mouth like it came out of him and he didn't mean to say it. I looked past it because the nurse had just walked in. She asked if I was feeling better and that I would be going home. She told me that my family was coming to get me.

I honestly do not know how long I was in the hospital or how long I was asleep. When the nurse came to give discharge instructions for my family and I, she stated that the only thing in my system from the tox screen was marijuana.

When I arrived at my parents' place I headed straight to my old bedroom. I talked to my family members from time to time when they wanted to check on me. My family from out of town would call and give me advice and instructions.

My grandfather told me, "Do not go down the street and hang with those guys from the neighborhood!"

My grandmother on my father's side told me, "Do not let your cousins or uncle and them come by and see you! Stay in your room until they leave when they do come by!"

I understood about the friends in the hood, but my own family, I didn't. I was glad that they were concerned though.

Chapter 12

My First Time Trying Recovery While at My Parents' House in the Old Neighborhood

I used to sleep most of the time. It got to a point that the only thing I wanted to do was sleep. I found myself having strong dreams. I had my first wet dream at that time. I couldn't believe that at the age of twenty-four, I had my first wet dream. I was in LA in the dream, and my LA homey from school brought a female for me to kick it with. I was in the dream having sex with a Cali bitch! She had a certain glow about to signify that she was of Cali breed with a nice body shape and hairy trimmed vagina and nice, bouncy, firm titties. She had brown skin with the Afro puffs. We were kicking it, and I started having sex with her. I looked out the window while we were having sex and saw my LA homeboy giving me the thumbs-up. I started to come as I continued to stroke up on her. At the same time, I was coming in her in the dream. I woke up and my penis was shooting out come. It kinda hurt. I mean, it wasn't an unbearable pain but more of a stinging discomfort. I reached down, and the come was thick like a milkshake. I went to the restroom, and it was a discolored ejaculation as well. It had more of a color of butter pecan ice cream. It was a bunch. It had my draws sticky. I couldn't believe it. I had a wet dream at my age and a strong one at that. I think it had something to do with my senses being open from the trauma I just experienced.

Most often, my thoughts were on getting back at the ones who put me in this situation. It was like I knew who they were, but they had helpers that I didn't know about. I didn't know who were involved and knew the activities that took place. My dreams were of a smiling emoji face in the sky. It would take me all over the world. Each time, it would either destroy or help someone. The ones that it would destroy were so-called friends from school or my hood home-boys. The traveling to other countries were more of a helping nature. Those were still hard to understand, but all I knew was that the smil-ing yellow emoji face was supposed to be God and his help for me.

The dreams of help and help against my considered enemies weren't the only things I saw while asleep and trying to sleep. I saw demons as well. One time, I had seen a black figure of a bull's head with a human body on the side of the bed on the wall. It was pump-ing his fist in the air like it was rooting on me. Then all of a sudden, I was wrestling with it. I was yelling and cursing at it. I was yelling, "You still can't kill me, motherfucker! I'm still here, bitch!" Then it grabbed my privates and was squeezing my nuts. I had an illusion of me walking in the bedroom, yelling at it, and addressing it as if it were in the air. I felt good about that because I felt that I was getting stronger.

I would get a call from my ex-girlfriend from college that she didn't act like she cared too much about my health. I guess because before I had the breakdown at the apartment, we had gotten into it. She thought that I was acting strange and called my mother. The bitch called my mom right in front of me. I couldn't believe it. I was pissed and ready to spit on her for that. When she would call me, she would talk of having sex, but it wasn't necessarily with me. She spoke of some penis that she wasn't going to be able to get anymore. My sister answered the phone, and I think she was still listening because as soon as she was done saying it, I heard her come to my door in the hallway. I heard a voice from her but don't know if it was her because I didn't see her though the door. I heard her say, "She trying to make his penis small!"

As soon as I heard that, my ex was willing to go back to the apartment and lay up with me. When I planned to pick her up from her parents' house, I was walking out of my bedroom door, and when I walked by my parents' bedroom, I saw my father watching TV on the edge of the front of the bed. When I walked past, I saw him wave his hands in front of him as to say he didn't want me or that he didn't want me to go. We made it to my apartment, and we were getting ready for bed. My penis was hard and showing through my drawers. I asked her if it look smaller. She said it looked bigger. We laid on the bed, but we didn't have sex. I wanted to play with her and wake her up to some dick or turn her on from out of her sleep.

As we lay there, the sky through the window had gotten red again. I heard a voice say, "You killed my child," but the message was clear that the kid I was supposed to have with this woman was to be the son of the devil. I don't know how I came to that conclusion, but that was the information I got from it.

I laid there in deep thought, thinking about what it all meant. I tried to get some rest, but I kept feeling my penis getting snipped. Every time it would grow back, but then there would be a snip from back at the base of my penis. I wasn't hard or turned on or anything, but I felt each and every snip and heard every scissor sound. It must have happened over fifty times. I dozed off still getting snipped in my sleep, or at least I would wake up from time to time and it would still be going on. Then I felt a hot sensation coming over my entire body. It was like the heat was creeping up on me. My ex-girl had moved her foot and placed it on my ankles and legs from time to time, and the hot fuzzy sensation on my body would go away every time she did it. She looked asleep to me, and it seemed to be done on accident, but I wasn't trusting shit not a damn thing.

When the heat got too hot for me, she didn't move her leg or foot to protect me. That was what I thought she was doing, then I quickly thought that she was just getting her issue. Since she said she was blessed and all, I felt that her fucking other niggas and my homeboys and being involved in their skits from early years and set-ups wasn't a blessing, and I hoped that they were all dead. I didn't know what she was hearing or what was on her mind. I didn't know if she was asleep, and it was some kind of intention of her to help me from the overcoming heat sensation or not. I didn't know if it was something she had planned and that was why she considered herself blessed. I didn't know what to think. All I knew was that I was pissed and willing to claim all my intuitions and not give a fuck about nobody. It was like they caused the heat and was to bail on me when they were done. I felt was that she wasn't doing the leg thing every time and left me burning hot like a motherfucker.

I really didn't get any sleep. I dozed off twice and woke up to scissors. I must have been snipped more than one hundred to two hundred times once the night was over. I dropped her off at her parents' house an hour away from the apartment. I wasn't upset that we didn't have sex; I was glad because I thought I would have embarrassed myself with a little penis pecker. I made it home and went right back the bedroom to get some sleep.

I was slowing down on seeing and being stuck seeing the strong illusions and hallucinations. I started to work out like my psychologist had suggested. I was supposed to take medicine. I was labeled an acute paranoid schizophrenic. I say "labeled" because I thought it was all a setup. Sure, I was seeing illusions and things, but I always did. I also had an ability to look past them even with the marijuana use.

I had visitors that came and would ask me what happened. I would tell them hoping it would be in confidence. A female friend from high school came by and joked with me about having a friend attached to me. That bitch! The nerve of her making a li'l statement like that. I felt I should have slapped the light skin off her li'l flat ass when she walked away. My homeboy who I used to go riding looking for hoes with mentioned something about smoking dope. I didn't see him say it, but I heard it, and it was said with a giggle. I didn't care if it was an illusion or not, but it held weight on me. I told myself at that point that I would never ever do any drug greater than marijuana. I didn't want to be seen and known as someone who was a crackhead or a serious drug addict.

My ex-girlfriend even called me and asked me to marry her. I didn't accept. I thought she heard of me going to the social security office and applying for disability benefits. She graduated, but her degree wasn't a solid 36,000-per-year paycheck; it was more like a

22,000-per-year degree before taxes. I felt she was a real bitch for that, asking a nigga to marry her after all that bullshit she was on. I felt more and more like the setup was being manipulated to more and more real-life issues, and they were going to be played out no matter what my situation or condition was. These MFs were fiending to get their issues like things was funny for real. I felt like pissing and spitting on everybody.

I got back in contact with my high school friend who I used to have a relation with. We were getting information and things about each other to further our relation. When her boyfriend and baby daddy found out of her being back in contact with me, he asked her to marry him. She called me, so excited of telling me the news. The only thing I could think was that I had motherfuckers handcuffing their broads for real. I had niggas getting married to save their relationships from me. It felt good to think. I had already been getting more and more witty and sarcastic against the sickness and the illusions that were trying to belittle me. She came over and had sucked my dick while we were getting to know each other again. I wanted to say it to her for him to hear when she called and told me, but I kept it G and congratulated her.

I would go to the doctor's appointments with my family, and it was like they had more to say than I did. I was the one going through the shit. I tried to explain that to everyone in the room during the appointments, but they would all answer, "You are not alone! We are all with you. We are all affected!" At that time, I couldn't understand fully what they meant. It was like there was something for them to say in a time like that to keep themselves involved with my shit, so they would have right to act or speak like it was in my behalf. I really didn't feel that they were on my side at all and was just so-called supporting me to look good. I really didn't feel that they knew what I was going through, and I started to suspect them thinking that they knew what I was going through and the setup, which I called the "granular annular" from my early years and the community. I heard a voice from my father saying that I wasn't God during one of the appointments. I wanted to yell at the nigga and say, "Bitch, I didn't say I was God! And just 'cause I came from yo' nuts don't make you him either!" I didn't talk too much most of the times at the doctor's appointments. I let them talk and eventually told the doctor I wanted appointments by myself with him.

I started to feel that my immediate family in my parents' house wasn't in my favor and were combative to me and my decisions. I wasn't going to visit the homies, and to me, that was all that mattered to some of them. It seemed as though I had an effect on the hood. One time while walking on the treadmill in the attic by the side window, going hard working out, I looked and saw a dark-skinned hood rat that was walking down the street with two of her friends. I saw her look back at her girls. As soon as I looked closer, she made a gesture of holding her hands in front of her forehead in a *C*-like gesture, and her fingers were touching her forehead like she was holding a cup in front of her head. It was like she was giving up, thinking something… My first thought was that I was getting better, and the talk in the hood, if any, had a lot of people in the hood thinking differently about my situation. I wasn't around to see them acting funny, them trying to embarrass me, or me being embarrassed about a nervous or mental breakdown and having to leave school.

My sister was counting my pills and confronted me one time in front of the rest of the family. She seemed more jealous than upset from my first thought. All I knew is that she was mad, and what she said at the time didn't make any sense. She said, "You ain't even been taking your meds! You been driving up and down the freeway and ain't even been taking your meds!" The way she said it was very sarcastic and nasty. I was just like *Fuck you* to her in my head. I thought she was mad because I was still doing what I wanted to do and not what the family and everyone else wanted me to do. I was urged by my parents, especially my father, to keep taking the meds and let them get in my system. I was told and kept being told that it would take time for them to start working. I never thought that they would work. I didn't take them too often. I never thought that I was sick for real.

Back to School for Classes for the First Time after Recovery

I decided to go back to school and live in the same apartment where I had the nervous/mental breakdown. I couldn't enroll in school at the time I returned. I was better than from when I first crashed, but I wasn't 100 percent done with recuperating. I got a job at a local discount store. I worked in the furniture department. I saw girls from school go up there, look at me, smile, and some would ask if I was graduating soon. Some girls I've never seen before would go in and place their hands on the counter with their fingers spread. The only thing I could seem to think was that they were Vice Lords or Bloods. I didn't think that they had a beef with me or knew what I was involved or affiliated with to even come and represent me, but you never know who would be talking your name or for what reason.

I had trouble paying rent for the first time in that apartment. I just wasn't making enough from the job and missed my hustle and legal income of the financial aid checks and the on-campus employment. I asked my grandfather for some help with rent. He agreed to send me $300. I didn't think that he would though, but he did. I didn't think he would because right before I got sick, I talked to him and my grandmother on the phone that time. Since my father was pissed, like on the "how dare you" level, then, I thought they were all still upset with all my decisions. My grandfather sent the 300, and I took care of rent, but I was sick of that store job. I met a couple of females who wanted to kick it after work to smoke and drink, but I didn't have enough to smoke with myself at the time. I still had my real gold medallion and fake chain and gold hoop earrings, but I was broke as fuck.

Once school started, I quit the store job and started receiving school grant reimbursement checks, which caught me up on my bills. I wanted more though. I sold guns small time in the previous two years while in the apartment. I started hustling them again. I was still a small-timer, but I had gotten a chance to get my old campus job back too. So things were looking up. While selling guns before I got sick, I sold some guns to niggas in the hood. I also sold some guns and made connections with other people in state and out of state. I gave them free guns and some cash that they could get things started with as far as business ventures if they stacked up more on it.

I did this because I wasn't trusting of the people I was around with and came around and knew that I would come around. I basically paid for protection, but it was really for revenge if I had gotten killed. Everyone knew I had guns for sale, and some used to come up to me with their hands, asking for a low price. Some I looked out for and others I sold cheap, like the 5 Star nine-millimeter semiautomatic handguns. Nothing was really a big operation. I just knew that I couldn't do it like the White boy and buy a house with the hustle money because I felt I was hot from everyone's setup and questions of what was going on with me.

I started classes, and things were going good for a while. It was like freshman year all over again. I could feel the unfamiliarness of the things around more. I didn't recognize and I didn't see the same people as I did before. I had only been gone for three months, and I thought the same people should have been around. It was like I couldn't catch up with anyone that used to be on campus. I thought to myself that it didn't matter; the goal was to get back in the swing of going to classes.

I didn't come across anyone I knew from when I was on campus previously, and I would be in my apartment just bored. I didn't drive anywhere. I didn't get any boppers or prostitutes. I just went to campus, but it became harder and harder to study. Every time I tried to concentrate at home to study or in class, I would just go blank. It wasn't a dark blank, but it was more like just stuck in thought. I couldn't gather myself to do what I was supposed to do.

I decided to go back home. I withdrew from classes. My father and I went back to clean the apartment out. I knew that I was supposed to graduate, and I didn't want to fail at it. I said that I would be back. I had just started to get my disability benefits.

I decided that when I got back to the hood that I was going to see what was going on with the hood. I was interested and was wondering what I was missing and what to further keep away from.

Chapter 14

Back in the Hood after First Return to School

When I came back, I came to the click house almost every day. Every day, we would smoke. Every day was just another day of smoking. I would wait for my homey Hank who went to junior high with me and who would come down to visit from time to time. He worked and everyone else hustled. I would see them sometimes during the day. When they would see me, all they wanted was a ride or some kind of favor. I used to give them rides, and I would look so silly. I would be so deep with niggas in the car that I looked like an old lady squashed up in the front seat. Sometimes I could barely turn the wheel. When it was time to ride with them and hit some corners, smoke, and kick it, they mostly would say that they were deep, but there would only be another one or two passengers. I used to feel funny about it, but it was really because I didn't have my own place to smoke yet and didn't want to drive and smoke in my car. It was cool, though; it gave me a better understanding of my position with them, and I was still seeing them as victims from what they had done to me. The more they acted funny toward me, the more they hid their li'l function, the more strength I would receive.

It was all right giving rides from time to time. I didn't have anything else to do. Plus, I was spying on niggas. I wasn't spying to snitch on them or anything but to get a better understanding of what the fuck they were really on and were about. I was on one with them for real. I mean, most times things were good because we were all smoking, but from time to time, they would try and OG a nigga like they were something for real. I used to abide and laugh at them like they were bitches when it was over. I got addicted to clowning on them and thought they were silly faggots.

If I wasn't going down the to the click house, I was at home recuperating from still having my mind fall and being sick. I was starting to take the medicine more and more, but it never seemed to work. I would be tripping hard at my parents' home. It would last from the time I laid down to the time I woke up; I would either be laughing while seeing illusions and hallucinations or feeling pain and restlessness from seeing them. The only time I didn't see too many illusions was when I was around the homies in the hood. I guess 'cause I was on one and I didn't have time to. I further felt that the difference in mental awareness and the despairing difference in the amount of illusions and hallucinations from the click house and the hood compared to my parents' house was a setup too. I guess I was too trusting in the hood and not my family. I really didn't trust either.

My behavior was still in order to get back to school. I kept seeing illusions at my parents' house. It got to the point where I would look in the mirror and say that I hated myself and then quickly turn around and say that I loved myself. It was like the sickness had its own identity. I never honestly thought that I was sick for real. It was me against the thing. I knew that my hood homies, school homies, the community, and anyone else I considered a contributor to my condition was winning because I had started hating myself, but I could never keep that thought in my head. Something else and I was always telling me that I would get through it and that I had to win that part of me that was gaining the identity of myself and going against and hurting me.

It seemed as though every time I went around the homies, things got easier and easier to deal with in my situation. I would often wonder why when I was around them, I never had any illusions or episodes. It seemed as though it was planned for me to be against the people who were closer to me. My parents and family would always question my behavior. The hood homies never did, but really, they just didn't to my face.

I gave them something to talk about while with my homeboy who I went to high school with from the hood. Once while we were riding to pick up a female he was about to fuck. I just started tripping. I was acting like I was a guard dog. I started seeing and hearing stuff from other cars that just made me want to react more. I didn't mind acting like that because I wanted her to know that I was crazy and would get bout for my nigga if someone tried him. It later turned to me being in public with him and him putting me on front a street a couple of times. He would tell me in public, "Let them know who you was with!" I felt funny every time I was asked. I felt like I didn't have to say it. I also felt funny because I was always told who someone was or told a name of someone in the hood like I knew the person. I didn't know those motherfuckers for real. I was just meeting the niggas in the hood, but they already knew me.

I would wonder what they had known me for though. Did they know me for what Sylvester had said that I wasn't down for my niggas because I kicked him and his boy out of my establishment at school for stealing and other shit? Did they know me from the old hood incident early in the hood with me pulling out my penis and things that stemmed from that? Did they know me as a schoolboy fuck boy to get played and preyed upon, or did they know me as others knew me that were away from the hood? Did they know me as a nigga that was looking out for the hood, even though some core homies were on bullshit with me? Did they know me as an initiator of music making in the hood? Did they know me for selling guns to the hood and looking out for homies when they came to town despite what Sylvester and I went through knowing he was a hoe-ass weirdo nigga?

I don't know what they thought or knew really; I just didn't fuck with too many niggas from the hood but gave respect and kept it G, kept it moving to whatever mission I was on. I didn't feel that I had to show extra love and come out of my character to show off to or for niggas. I felt that that wasn't G like, and it definitely didn't fit me even though I enjoyed the crazy stigma that I was given to a point.

That point being bringing my family and others who were and could be seen as authority to me to an issue or concern about me.

It was okay when I was in the hood with the homies. It wasn't all bad. We used to have fun, talking of old school-age times in the hood, smoking weed, and partying. I went on a gangster party with one of the older homies and his girls. He told the girls I was from my school city, but I spoke up and let them know where I was really from. I never did not claim my home city. I was proud of where I was from and never wanted to lie about where I was from; it just didn't feel right. I was the first to get sex that night. It was some head from one the older homey girls that he said he picked up from the grocery store. While the girl was giving me head, he was just behind her and was fucking her doggy style. While she was sucking, Hank came down from upstairs, and I heard him say he straight.

I guess he was talking about my dick size and that I could still function after what I had been through. Fraizer was there watching while I got served and threw the hood gang sign up. When I first started to recover at home, he called my family house and spoke with me, saying, "We just like you!" Further saying, "We all in the same situation!" I couldn't take what he was saying to weight, but later I got a sense of comfort being around the hood homies even though I knew they were still on bullshit and I was still on one too. I smoked and chilled and learned a couple of things about the environment that my homeboys were talking about. They did everything together, but me, I did everything by myself. I still never told them that I did some gunplay while down at school. I was just peeping game on niggas. My mind would never let me believe that I was sick, even though I was taking the meds and all.

I knew that I made my mother scared of me, and my family was starting to see me more as a black sheep. That was what I would think. I really didn't give a fuck about what people said, but it seemed more now that I always had to defend my behavior or how I was perceived. I cared of what they thought most times because I wanted to keep them away from asking questions. I wasn't doing anything productive for real. I was just hanging with the wrong people. In hood rules, I was hanging with the right people though. I still didn't like how there were no serious illusions or hallucinations around the person who went through my safe and possibly worse. My family was always there for me, and I knew it. The community wasn't there for me like my family, but the community, as long as I was involved with it, had my back on li'l things but not bigger.

They would help with li'l things like a flat tire or helping out in situations like that or if something happened directly in the hood. But with bigger things, they wouldn't but would love to hear about that type of stuff. I called Hank one time and his father answered. He told me, "I see you done went down there and got your head big!" I knew then exactly what was on the minds of the people and families in the community. I was pissed that this nigga old man would go like that. I felt embarrassed more for him and people in the community more than being ashamed or embarrassed about what happened to me. That gave me more motivation to keep up my antics of not letting things slide with the hood homies or the community as a whole. Fuck them!

C h a p t e r 1 5

Returning to School to Give the Old College a Try

I decided it was time to go back to school. I called my ex-roommate Lavar. I was looking for a spot to save a disability checkup before I got into my own place. He told me it was cool to stay with him until I got my first month rent and deposit together. I told him he could son me, being silly about his New York accent and his New York ways. He was staying with Greg, one of the suspicious Freaknik niggas. They were Masons now. They all were.

My LA homie was one that I should have called, but the incident of kicking him and his roommate Stag out once prevented me from calling him for that favor. They were also Masons, and I thought they didn't have time for it and didn't want to be involved with helping me again, even though we kept in touch. I don't know if they still felt funny about things or not, but I guess I did. I was supposed to let them stay at my place with me before I got sick. They let me stay with them when I was between apartments, but when they stayed with me, I couldn't take it. They had their stuff over at my place, but I didn't give them a key to get back and forth. They didn't give me a copy when I stayed with them. I thought that there was a certain amount of respect and rules when someone was letting you stay with them. I felt that they had broken those rules. They had been over a girl's house playing cards or so they said. They kept calling, waking me out of my sleep. They kept saying that they were on their way.

Every time they called, they kept saying the same thing. I was like, "Damn, if them niggas coming, then come and stop waking me up with these damn phone calls every couple hours, yelling in my ear about it." The second to last time they called, I saw their faces through the phone. It was an illusion, and I did not appreciate the way I saw them smiling through the phone, and the annoyance of them yelling through the phone just didn't sit well with me. Then after the last call, they didn't come till another two hours later, and it had me twisted. When they knocked on the door, something came over me. I started crying like a li'l girl. My eyes were so tight from all the marijuana and coming in and out of sleep that I just ran to the door crying. I opened it and ran back into the bedroom. My LA homie asked me through the door what was wrong; he kept asking me and asking me. I just went to sleep.

The next day, they decided for themselves to stay with someone else. They were acting like they were shocked and disgusted by my reaction at the door. I wasn't though. Honestly, I was glad that they left and was willing to go. So I didn't really want to stay with any Masons who didn't even include me in a process of joking and kept things a secret from my African friend and me. It was like we were not to be included on purpose, but it was a way to go up real quick and get settled again before classes started.

I stayed in the basement of Lavar and Greg's town house. We were doing the same thing again as before; we were smoking and playing video games. They never smoked around their kids, and I understood that it was a good thing. I would be in the basement sometimes while they had company, and my mind would trip. The voices that were from upstairs to the basement would turn into thoughts of something else than what they were talking about, and I would have illusions of personal things in my life. The voices and illusions would start to coincide with each other to the point where all I heard was the voices coming from upstairs, like they were tellin' me and commenting on my personal business and thoughts. I would see shadow illusions on the wall of my father with his arms crossed like he was watching over me. Another night I saw a shadow illusion of my homeboy Hank doing the same thing, like he was also watching over me.

I got in my own place a street away from Lavar and Greg's. It was a nice one-bedroom flat. It was long and had a front and back door with a wood sliding door separating the living room from the bedroom, which was in the middle of the flat. I had plenty of fun in that apartment and plenty of problems as well, both mentally and with my property. In this apartment, I had much more active gangster activity brought about by me as a result of mental health issues, school success, and personal-relations issues.

I was working with Lavar and Greg as a youth specialist at a children's home. During that time, I experienced an awakening, an ability of energy transfer. While working with some of the youths in a group that I was monitoring, one of the youths was throwing a basketball at the other youths in line while I was gathering them to leave. He wouldn't follow instructions, and I had to restrain him. I started to restrain him, and he tried to struggle with me. I held him up against the wall. He fainted and I let him down to the floor. All the other kids were scared. I said something in tongues and snapped my fingers over him. I do not know what I said, but he quickly woke up from wherever he had been. He was shaken up, and his parents wanted me to go to court for my actions toward their son. I was found not guilty in court. The judges had me wait till they heard all the cases for the day, and when it was time for my case to be heard, they said that I was just doing my job.

The incident of the youth and court had me thinking of when after I went back to school the first time after getting sick. I went to a church to seek advice from a local pastor in my school city. I also previously went to church to seek advice and help from a preacher at my old grade school church. I went to service, and all I could do was cry. It wasn't a weeping cry but tears kept coming down my eyes during the entire service.

The church I visited in my school city was Baptist and mainly Black. I sat waiting to talk to him, and I saw a picture in the hallway right outside of the room that I was waiting for the pastor at. The picture was of a Black, young male who had different colors for each extremity. One shoulder was imperfect from the other, and one leg was longer than the other. At the time, I was just thinking Africanism and the aspect of it taking a community to raise a child. I thought that the picture was of how every aspect of the community had a say in raising the child, and the young man was perfectly imperfect not necessarily raised by one mother and father and their knowing but was pieced up by everyone in the community. That was the answer that popped up from what I saw when I looked at the picture. It thought again as I thought of what happened with the youth at my job. Looking back on the picture had me thinking more of Christ and his ability to use more of a percentage of his brain and do miracles. How the two views of the picture came, I do not know. I didn't want to think too special of myself, but I was interested in the origin of Jesus and the truth, if any, of his existence.

While working at the youth home, I received a call. It was my sister crying, saying that my grandfather had passed. I didn't know what to say to her to calm her down and make the situation easier for both of us. I made plans with my job to go to the funeral. I had missed my great-grandfather's funeral, and I think my family was upset with me for a while because of it, but after a while, I got used to accepting my thought of leaving him as a great man in memory and not saying goodbye. I didn't want to miss my grandfather's funeral though. He had adopted my father and married his mother, who is my biological grandmother. He was a good man, and I respected and loved him. He was always available to talk to and was easy to talk to. He was available when my father wasn't. My father worked hard to keep us on a certain level of knowing in economics and having some nice things for us, but we rarely talked about father-and-son issues. He always tried to make sure I didn't get my ass in big trouble. I loved my grandfather dearly. He could always talk like a player and bring a smile to my face. We were close from the $300 he gave me for rent to the times as a child talking and kidding with him as he injected himself with insulin for his diabetes in the back breakfast room when they came to visit.

When I came back from the funeral, I missed a couple of training and testing dates that were essential in me keeping the job, so I was told. I thought that the pressure of the young man's family that wanted me to go to court for the gym incident had started to hold weight. I lost that job and was feeling devious against White people in the city, but I didn't take anything out on them. The victory that I thought they had only lasted for a minute as I started to turn back to doing hustle scams and started robbing people.

Things slowly started going bad for me. I was getting money in as usual, and I had purchased a new used car that I put on Dayton rims on. The rims were fifteen-inch Dayton racing wheels on Vogue Tyres. I had a stack knob stereo system with tape and CD. It was an upgrade from the Chevy Beretta, which was totaled from an accident on the freeway going to my home city with my young homie who needed a ride there. He blamed everything on himself, saying he was bad luck. I didn't mind what he was saying. During that short period of time with him, I didn't have any illusions or hallucinations. I needed to get rid of the car anyway because I had been riding around, hunting for licks and did a couple robberies from that car. I might not have been seen driving the car because I would park, get out, and go on foot, but the victims or snitches might have noticed me pulling from the area, bumping sounds.

Mental Health, School Career, and Relations at My Second Solo Apartment in My School City

I did criminal activity in both the cars I had during my return to the schoolyard and living in the city. I met girls who gave me play just because I was on Daytons. I was still tricking, and I would mess with regular broads too. I would go riding just to find girls and get numbers, and then I would go riding just to find hoes.

One girl came by the next day after giving her number. I had grilled some meats and had some weed and wine coolers. We had sex that same night. She had seven kids, and her sex game was okay at first. I shot two shots into her. I was tripping because it was an irregular nut that I had busted. It was just two quick squirts from my dick in her. She spent the night, and I caught her looking at me while I was asleep. I thought it was unusual not because she was looking but because of the position that I was sleeping in when I woke up and caught her. I had my arms and elbows crossed while I was facing the bed and holding me up; my legs crossed together at the knees and ankles. I saw her roll over. But it was an illusion of her rolling over. I mean, it was a cartoon and she looked like steams of colors and lights, like a ghost. The next time I woke up in the morning, she had started sucking my dick as soon as my eyes opened. Then she jumped on top, and my penis felt like a long snake growing inside her as she bounced on it. It only lasted for a minute. My penis got soft, but it was still long from her touch and being inside her.

We lost contact after seeing each other a couple more times after that. I remember the last time she came over, I was in my robe, and she felt like I wasn't being nice to her. I didn't give a fuck though. I had plenty of girls in that apartment. I remember seeing illusions while listening to DMX's "Ruff Ryders Anthem." I saw on my couch an illusion of a girl twerking. It was a white cartoon, like a small ghost, just big enough to fit as a picture on the part of the couch where a person lay his back against. I saw the illusion and I started imagining it getting stroked by me, and I saw it being done as a small ghostly cartoon. I saw many different illusions in that apartment, but they were controllable.

It was so easy for me to see an illusion or hallucination and have it do what I wanted it to do or be. Sometimes it would challenge me, and other times it would just go along with what I wanted to see. The ability to control or convert the illusions started from being in my bedroom at my parents' house when I was recuperating. I was laughing and was in pain, but I was learning how to bend light and studying light and how they would bring the ability to see illusions and hallucinations easier.

In this apartment, I had a pet pit bull I bought from a guy I bought some weed from. When I went to pick out the dog, they only had females left, and I wanted a male. When I chose her, the drug dealer wife yelled something to the dog, but I didn't hear it. I mean, she was right in front of me, and I saw her face struggling while she was saying it like she was yelling in the dog's face, but nothing came out of her mouth or at least I didn't hear it. I thought she put a hex on the dog. I thought she told the puppy to misbehave. I took the dog home, and it didn't want to eat; it wouldn't walk with me, and all it wanted to do was sit on my shoulder like a parrot while I was watching TV.

I was still going home on some weekends, and I would leave the dog with my young neighbors across the street. My neighbor next door came by, and we smoked a blunt. She was cool, I thought. A young White girl from another state. When she left, my dog ran to the window, and an illusion of the li'l puppy's brain inside her head was turning really fast and being rattled around really quick. The dog was comfortable in my place and had food but barely ate. I heard the TV Man say, "You just sitting there with your parrot!" When I saw the dog's head get rattled at the window, I heard the girl's voice who stayed next door say, "You rattled his head a li'l bit!" like I had done it. It still felt good having a pet around.

The guy who I tried to kill after I took him home had gotten back in contact with me. He came by and brought a can of grown dog food. We wanted to smoke, but I didn't have any weed. I told him the guy I bought the puppy from had weed. He stayed four to five streets over. We started to walk over there. When we got there, the drug dealer sold us the sack, and the guy I was with kept starting to have conversations with him. It was funny because the drug dealer just kept shaking his head back and forth while he was being talked to. He didn't answer the guy or nothing. He was just shaking his head in a sequence motion with his head directly in the face of Herm—a nigga I wanted to kill and went looking for, as if to say, "No, not today. Be gone with all that shit."

While we were walking back to my apartment, I stepped into some gritty mud. It was all on my left foot. When I got back to my apartment, I didn't wash my foot right away. Later it developed into thick toenails that looked like thick fungus. I got it tested, and I was told it was just thick nail, but why was it just on that foot that stepped on the gritty mud on that rainy night?

I had plenty of girls come by. Some boppers and some regular girls. The regular girls seemed to just want to be fucking friends, and the boppers inquired about linking with me long term as in a relationship. One girl, while I was stroking her, said "Eric is the master of the universe!" I felt funny because she was a bopper, and I never told her my name. It was like that, I would give them fake names half of the times. Either they would leave a note on my car or walk up to the car when I was in it. The Dayton spoke a lot to 'em, even some niggas wanted to drive and kick it. One even tried to play like it was his car, asking me to not say anything when he told them it was his car. I hated that; I didn't know that motherfucker like that.

He told me he was a Crip, I guess thinking that I would feel him or feel some type on camaraderie with him. I just thought he was a bum for asking me some shit like that. He would come by a lot, acting like we were cool. It seemed to me like he wanted me to trust him, but I couldn't. This was the same guy who, when I was high and dozing off, was outside in the early mornings and late nights, keeping up noise. I went out there in my robe and asked them to turn down the noise. He was the brother or cousin of the actual resident who stayed a couple doors down with his girlfriend. I had smoked a blunt and flirted with her when she brought up some troubles about her dude. I didn't know if he was trying to win my trust and rob me or put me in a crazy situation or not.

I was mentally healthy enough for me to make it to classes and work. I had fun kicking it in the city streets, flossing on rims and bumping sounds and meeting and having sex with the different types of women. I was seeing a doctor, who prescribed me Haldol. It was a different medicine from the previously prescribed Stelazine and Cogentin. I had strong side effects from the Stelazine, so they changed prescriptions. The Haldol didn't work either. The only thing that helped me was marijuana. It helped me see the illusions for what they were and manipulate them easier with the knowledge I had acquired from studying myself while at my parents' home. I would see so many different things from after giving my dog medicine and him throwing it up and seeing a skull coming from the vomit to rappers like DMX spitting on the side up in my head and me physically feeling it. All in all, I would just keep doing what I was doing, which was school, work, and home protection.

I had another neighbor who stayed under me. His apartment was in the basement. He was a White older guy, and it seemed like he had been living there forever because of all the books and news clipping around. He was cool though. He told me that he had seen someone outside my side window of the bedroom, looking in. I was upset because I just recently had been masturbating on the bed one night, and when I was done, I heard someone yell from the window, "Don't forget those people!" When it was said, I recognized the face of the voice but didn't see who said it. It sounded and looked like my hood friend Jabral, who I lent my gun to on a visit before. I wasn't sure if it was him or not. I didn't know why he would even be down here and especially at my window, except for to be on some hating shit. When it was said, I saw colors of all types and supposed to be wind and chaos coming through the window. I knew it was an illusion, but I just didn't feel like getting up and getting active to attempt to confront whoever was at the window. That was how I was and continued to be for a while. I would see an illusion or have a hallucination and just let it be. I did this because the doctors were always concerned if I wanted to harm myself or others. I knew that they just cared if I was trying to hurt others, or at least that was how I felt.

I was seeing so much it was like I was starting to see things that I would see in the future. I would see things that would happen later on in my everyday life. I attributed it to my mind being able to see more than just what my eyes concentrated to see. I knew that the mind is always working, and my senses are always on. My mind would analyze a situation from seeing the same thing I was seeing with my eyes but seeing more and connecting the dots to what would be possibly an alternative action, reaction, or situation. Once I saw a White man flying pass my window with a long, long black penis. I never understood what it truly meant except that I was about to graduate, and I knew that it was hate for me, and the want for me to fail was great.

While going to classes, I would feel the hate from others, not just the Whites but people of different races. It would calm down once I got to my classes, and I would once again be the first to raise my hand and answer and ask questions. I was hoping to get my GPA up in my last two quarters of school. I had classes scheduled like basketball and tennis. I scheduled the classes to bring my GPA up, plus I needed credits. The only classes I needed to graduate were two stats classes. Everything else were fillers to bring my GPA up.

One class was a gimmick class of ethnicity. I forgot the name and number of the class, but the professor wanted us to write a paper of our ethnic food and a meal. I wrote a paper on the New Year slave meal of pork, green leafy vegetables, and black-eyed peas. I explained in the paper what each portion of the food meant in my ethnic background and tradition. I received an *F* for the paper with an explanation that slavery wasn't an ethnicity. I tried to tell her that I didn't have a country that I came from to write a national dish about.

This was the only meal that my kind of people could and would adhere to. I noted to her that the paper included the history of slavery and the oppression that turned my people to eat the type of foods that were allowed and how we embraced them and used what we could in necessity and meaning. The explanation was turned down by her, and my grade remained an *F* for the paper. I was very upset at the fact of the grade and the effect it would eventually have on my GPA. I reported her to the ombudsman's office after I talked with some other students, one of which was a basketball player. He let me see his paper, and his paper was about some nonsense. I believe it was a rhyming fairy-tale-like thing. It had nothing to do with an ethnic dish. He received an *A* for his paper, and I received an *F* for a topic that the entire class was about.

While in the ombudsman's office, I sat and talked with the director of the school of the university. She walked in and sat behind me, and as I explained the situation to the director, she began to sniff like she was crying, but I really thought that she was full of shit. I further thought that she was trying to mess with my head, like she had information on me and my mental condition. I had stated to the doctors and to some others about certain sounds, like smacking of the mouth and such, that messed with my senses. I felt her as being a fake racist bitch like the girl with the black face who I almost shot falling out of my closet. I was instructed by the director to write a paper on a topic that I really don't remember, but it was harder than the original topic. I received a *C* for the entire class, and my grade point suffered. It was a reason for me to be asked to leave the school. I received a letter about my grades, GPA, and dismissal due to insufficient grades that violated a special probation financial aid situation. The grades were mailed to me, but that was not the actual reason why I had to leave school.

I had gotten into a fight on campus after riding down one of the streets on campus. While driving down the street, my mind was seeing thoughts on people as usual and me fading them as usual, but this time, a guy threw a rock at my car that almost entered my driver's side window; it felt like it hit my jaw. I quickly jumped out and ran up on the guy. He looked like a mix of an Arab and a White guy. I grabbed his arms and held him up against the step railings then socked him in the eye, leaving him with a bruise. He swelled up, and his eye colored quickly.

When I was walking away from him, I was flexing and yelling my name and told everyone watching to recognize and beware of me. I noticed a White guy holding a piece of paper up and giving me the thumbs-up. He wrote my license number down and the name I was yelling. I felt like it was a setup from the jump. I usually would see thoughts on people but never accepted them as anything major. This time, it was like I was set up to get in some type of trouble because the illusions were much stronger than before even though I could still fade it easily and keep it moving. This was the contributing reason I felt that it was also a racist reason I got kicked out of school and asked not to come back to campus. If I was a White boy, they would have just asked me to clean up the campus or something like that. I have a strong tendency to believe that my allegations of racism against a teacher, my look of how my lifestyle was, and rumors all had something to do with the decision to expel me from the campus. I was a nigga to them. A flashy gold-wearing, pants-sagging, large-body nigga. They didn't give a fuck about me and now me about them.

The fight didn't get me arrested by campus police, but I was called in to make a statement. The case went downtown, and I was put on probation and didn't even know what the charge was. I didn't even do any time, no handcuffs, no nothing. I was just sitting in court, and I was high. I was waiting for my case to be heard, and my father showed up. When it was time for my case to be heard, I was so high I didn't know what was going on. I didn't give a fuck though. School and all the glory of going to a big state school was over. I knew that a life change was coming from all the events that had happened. I didn't give a fuck what the next steps were at that point. I didn't get arrested, no cuffs, so I didn't think it was anything major, just a follow-up from the judiciary hearing that was on campus.

I didn't know why my father was there. I didn't invite him at all. I ended up having to pay a 250-dollar fine, and it was said to have been a probation fee only. I never understood why I had to pay a probation fee if I wasn't convicted of any crime. I was told it was just a misdemeanor and would not affect me getting a job in any kind of way. It was my first offense.

During the judiciary hearing on campus, the prosecutor for the school was strongly suggesting that I wasn't a good student and was a threat to the campus. I felt like I was being labeled a dirty nigga by him. I didn't get a chance to tell my side of the situation at all. I felt the process was fairly fine, and the way the White prosecutor for the school was always looking up to the ceiling or sky while making his statements just didn't feel right with me. I said to myself then if I was a threat to the campus and not being able to clean the campus or do some other type of community service for a small event, then I was going to be a campus terror then. All I knew was that it felt good beating him up. All I know was that I wanted more of that energy that got me kicked out and a reversal of that energy that got me a victim of a racist bitch. I wanted revenge for all the turmoil in my head, body, and my name from me just trying to make life better for myself and being mistreated by others.

I would sit in my apartment, and my money was getting low. No one came around anymore to visit. I told no one that I had gotten kicked out and that my grades didn't make it any better. It wasn't that I was ashamed. I just didn't want to hear anyone's voice talking about it, and I could imagine the ways that I would hear them. It was funny because while I was imagining the ways that I would hear them, there were no illusions or hallucinations to go with them.

I would sleep and have bad dreams again though, and at times, it would be of me coming out of my body and walking around the apartment and outside on the porch. I had those dreams before at the last apartment, after I came back from being sick, but I would never fully come out of my body at that point of the sickness. I would just see me breaking through from my forearms to my shoulders and head as to rise, but I would instantly wake up. I also had dreams of beings stuck in a place where I couldn't move and mostly everything was dark. Sometimes it was like my head was being pinned down. But no one was there. I saw shadows and images of ghosts that I thought were vampire-like entities. This happened at both apartments while in school.

I said it was time. I already had gunplay while at school, and it was time for some more. Every little thing, every little ping, every little light that tried to transform into something of an illusion that I thought came from an outside source, I was on it. I would jump up and go to the porch with my bat and search for whoever or whatever. I didn't consider myself sick in doing so. It felt too good. It had me feeling so good that while driving home one time, listening to a song that Tupac and Bone had collabed on, I heard Tupac say he still ain't said nothing, and it was in a way of praising me because I was doing crimes and I was not telling anyone. I didn't want to get caught, and I didn't want to fall a victim of snitching on myself.

Once while driving on the freeway, I denounced God and told him I hated him. I did it once, and when I calmed down, my chin lifted up, and I felt nectar dripping on my lips and into my mouth. The taste was that of sweet citrus. I later came to believe that God had blessed me for speaking my mind and not because I denounced him by yelling, "I hate you for what you have been doing to me!" Maybe it was the devil accepting my admission that God wasn't what I had known him or her to be and that maybe he really was dead like I was told on the night when I had my strong illusions.

At that time, I didn't know and didn't fully care until after coming back from my parents' place and sitting in my apartment that I felt water dripping on my forehead. I looked up and there wasn't a leak in sight. I went to bed shortly after that, and I had an illusion of bugs hanging over me on the wall. They were roaches and the biggest one was supposed to be like a representation of the group Wu-Tang Clan. It was right in the middle and on top of everything. I had a Bible next to my bed, and I began to read it. I opened it to Kings.

My LA homie told me he just had been reading Kings in the Bible, and I thought, well, maybe it was time that I did too. I opened it and started to read it. It was saying something about that which comes from mud will return to mud. I felt that nigga was a piece of shit for telling me to read that nonsense. Like he was trying to say something, like I was going to be nothing but a hood nigga over and over again. I got on my knees to pray, and I could not get up off my knees. I was stuck. I was pinned to the floor and the side of the bed. I kept telling myself I would never do this again, but I also stated that I would not be giving my soul to the devil either. When I was finally able to get up, I went straight to sleep.

The next evening, I wanted to go to my parents' house to get some money from my mom. I didn't have enough gas money to make it there. I went robbing just to get gas money to make it on the two-and-half-hour trip. I went around the campus area, parked my car, and got out on foot. I still had my jewelry on, and I tucked my chain and took my rings off. I tucked my chain under my sweatshirt and T-shirt to the point where you could not see any of it. I saw two White guys walking to the store. I ran up on them and asked them how much they had. One of them said, "Do you have a gun or something!" I pulled a nine, and they gave it up smoothly.

I made it to my mom's and got some money from her, about two hundred dollars. I robbed two White boys for forty dollars of their beer money just to make it home. I said to myself while driving back to my apartment from my home city that it was time to either stop robbing small-time stuff like what I had just done, get involved in bigger licks, or get a job. The apartment I was in was a good spot for only $425 with all utilities paid. I could afford that with an honest job and still have money left over to have fun with and save a little bit. My disability income would pay for my rent, bills, and food, but the extra money that I would get in was diminished. I wasn't robbing dope boys, but I did rob some people on a gang block before a time I was living at my previous apartment.

Once while driving on the freeway coming home to my apartment, I saw flashes of light from the sky. I was listening to Wu-Tang and Cappadonna. I had other music to listen to as well, but at the time, that was who I was bumping to. I saw live concerts in the sky. It was like the sky would open up, and I would see the rappers on the mic, rapping the songs that I was listening to. It was nighttime, and the sky would open up like a sliding window. I saw in full color and grandeur the show from the heavens. This illusion was not like the ones previous. It was like I was watching TV in the sky. While all these illusions were going on, I never once thought that I was sick and needed medication. I didn't feel I needed to hurt anyone; everything I was doing was for money. That would soon change.

Chapter 17

Trying to Live in the City and Relocating Back Home for a New Start

I had landed a job that was farther away from the campus. It was at a gas station. I was working okay as a cashier. We didn't have to stock because the vendors would come in once a week and fill and recycle everything. I was still at the same apartment, and I still had issues with people coming around my surroundings. The Crip nigga from a couple apartments down was still trying to come by and be friendly. He came over with his cousin or brother, whoever he was, that was the rightful leaser of the place where they were staying at. I made some cookies, and they were in the kitchen, eating some while I sat in the living room. I heard cousin, brother, or whatever his title was say, "Maybe he is starting to trust us!" That was all I heard, but I didn't need or want to hear anymore. I just knew that they were up to something. I didn't trust anyone or anything very, very strongly at that point in time. I couldn't trust my hood homies, my school homies, no bitches, my school, my parents, my neighbors, my dog, and my surroundings.

That MF Sylvester came down to visit shortly after the statement of the Crip nigga's brother, cousin, or whatever he was. I guess "the hood not fucking with me" statement was null to him since I had fallen that night and went home to recuperate. I never did forget the jerkish MF, and I was still on beam about every move he made. He came down with a nigga who he introduced as from my hood. I never knew him, but he would let me know that he didn't trust Sylvester either. Sylvester would leave from time to time and come back with a female or some weed or something. The newly introduced hood nigga got mad and left because Sylvester told him he was coming down to do something totally different than what he was doing, which was just sitting around with me.

Once I let Sylvester drive near campus while parties were going on. He was driving and I was in the passenger seat. I felt sensations on my penis like it was trying to grow. It wasn't getting hard, but I recognized what was going on with me. I kept my hand and finger on my thigh and was pulling my trigger finger toward my penis and was shooting the penis that was feeling the sensation of growing or maturing away. I was thinking to myself, *This MF ain't maturing me like he was an OG or something to me.* I kept shooting the new growth off over and over again. I don't know if that was what he trying to do or not—maturing me or harming me or what. But the illusion and even him being around me, I didn't want and got rid of. I switched to the driver's position, and he was in the passenger seat.

While driving, Sylvester began to get extremely close with his face damn near in my face. I was like, *Goddamn, this MF is an annoyance!* I started to see paper scrolls of writings coming down my eyes in front of my face. The illusion was strong, and it was hard for me to see and drive. I kept driving, ignoring the illusion, but it was still blinding me because of the orange color of the pages and the black writings on them. I didn't recognize the writings, and I didn't want to; I was making sure I wasn't about to get in an accident. That would have made this jerkish MF's evening. I wouldn't have stopped, hearing this story from the MF when he was around other people we knew.

The hood and I were still on different terms, and we all talked about each other behind our backs. An originator of the hood gang wanted to come to town and have fun at the parties that were going on around campus and in the city. While at home, he asked to go down with me, and he was going to bring some female friends of his too. I had been in contact with him during my time before I got sick in my last apartment at my school city. I wrote him while he was in one of our state correctional facilities. He called and we chopped it for a minute before the recording of the time had jumped in and cut the service. He was back in the hood, but from my knowledge, he was rarely seen. One time while riding with Tom and Fraizer, they kept telling me that James was a dummy. They were screaming, "Dumbass James!" It was so funny that I said it too while high and being silly.

James and I and the girls rode down to my old city school to kick it. I still had my apartment, but I didn't tell anyone yet that I was no longer a student. While driving down, I stopped at a gas station. When I went to the restroom, used the urinal, and proceeded to wash my hands, I saw in the mirror the picture of Mother Mary on my forehead. It was a full-body picture, and she was wearing blue garment robes and had red rosy lips. The outer shadow of the picture of the illusion was that of a light blue, which was fading outward to white. I knew it was an illusion and not a stamp on my head or anything like that. The girls in the back seat were flirting, but they never touched my forehead. While there, he wanted to go solo to the campus because I told him that I wasn't feeling good at that moment and wanted to rest. I gave him my nine-millimeter and the car keys and told him to be safe and be careful. He said he had a ball and came across a nigga from the home city who asked him if he needed a gun because he had two. James said he quickly told him, "Naw. I'm good, I got one already!" and showed it to him. Later on, James told me that other niggas in the hood told him not to come down here with me because I was off and I was crazy. I didn't feel upset from what James told me because I already knew what type of niggas they were. I had already been through so many incidents and bullshit with niggas in the hood that I wasn't shocked by them saying anything like that. I came to an understanding that once you learn how someone talks around and about others, they mostly likely will do the same about you and act that way toward you. I was glad that James had a great time.

The freeway and driving in the city was my way of releasing stress. I didn't always have to pull up on females and try to get numbers or flirt or whatever. Just the action of driving and being at peace with the music playing was great to me. My grandfather once told me that driving was my freedom, and I liked the way he said it to this day. Many times, I would drive and drive, and it seemed that every time I would stop and get gas or stop and use the restrooms and gas stations, I would feel something pulling at my legs. It was a hard pull from under my feet that also pulled at my hips. It was so painful that it would almost be crippling. I mean, my legs would hurt while I would walk afterward. I don't know if the devil was trying to pull me underground or not, but each time it hurt like hell. Half of the illusions had some type of physical pain to them. It seemed the more freely I moved about, the stronger the pull would be from that illusion and the more pain as a result of it. I felt like I was being enslaved and kept on earth because it only happened around White people at their respective locations.

Once while driving around by my job, I was followed by a White man who had his video camera on me. I was on the freeway, so I couldn't pull over and ask him to stop or yell at him like, "What the fuck are you doing?" or anything like that. I did pull over on a farther exit up the freeway and got something to eat and some gas. I remember thinking, *What the fuck is wrong with people?* I made it to my parents' house and slept for a couple of days with no illusions, and I haven't taken my medications in a long time, but I felt peaceful and energized.

I told my parents that I was giving up my apartment and wanted to get my things back up to home city and put them in storage. My father and older cousin were coming from down South at my granny's house. He previously told me that they would help me move and to meet them in the school city by the time they would pull up. I had my alarm set for a good time to get up, shower, and get dressed to make the trip with plenty of time. I heard the alarm and turned it off. I fell back to sleep. I kept saying I was about to get up but kept falling back to sleep.

My father called and asked where I was and that he was about three and half hours away from my school city. I told him I just got up, but I would still be on time to meet them. He instantly got mad and said, "It is over with! You will have to find someone else to help you move," and I heard my cousin call me a dumbass, saying it with my name like it was funny. I got off the phone like fuck them. I could have made it on time, but the Charlie MF was one who was always acting like he was in charge of things, acting all Charles in charge again. I felt like fuck him and that hoe-ass cousin he riding with, who was also my godfather.

The next couple of days, my cousin offered to ride with me to go get my stuff. We made it to the apartment, and I saw a U-Haul moving truck at one of the neighbors" house two apartments up the street. I knew something was funny. I walked to my apartment porch and saw the apartment door had been kicked in. I got inside and looked around. I saw all my stuff had been taken. My furniture, my bed, my plastic storage bin with my personal information like my Social Security number, and things were all gone. The most important thing out of all the stuff was my old-school-style chest that had my collection of music in it. I was pissed.

I walked to the U-Haul truck down the street and looked in it. I saw a bed inside of it that I thought was mine. One of the drivers of the truck asked what I was doing, and I got loud with him, asking whose bed that was and where they got it from. I didn't care that I was looking in their shit without their permission. They knew I was heated and told me that the Crip nigga had sold it to them. I further asked them about the rest of the stuff, and they said that they bought the bed and that they believe the couch was bought by someone on the next street. I called the police, and when they arrived, they told me that the Crip nigga already knew who he was and that he had warrants. I continued to give them information to make the theft and breaking and entering report. I told the officers that the White people who had my bed could keep it. I felt like they weren't going to get charged with accepting or buying stolen property anyways. They were White and the police didn't question them as if they did any crime anyways, even though I thought they were in on the theft of my stuff.

After my cousin and I pulled away from the police, I went straight to the Crip nigga's mama's house. I grabbed the gat and walked to the door. I knocked and knocked but no one answered.

I didn't hear anything going on inside or at the door. I was going to blast whoever came to door and jump on the freeway and go on with whatever consequence or life had in front of me. I am glad that no one answered because my cousin slash godfather was with me. I rarely, if at all, did anything as far as gunplay or violence with someone with me. I didn't know if he was going to snitch if we got caught, but at that time, I didn't care. I was gonna kill that nigga's mama or anyone that opened or came close to the door.

I made it home after speeding from being upset about my stuff and still being pumped from what I was about do and possibly go to jail for. All this time I had been a victim of people who were close to me or who had tried to get close to me. Yeah, I messed up a lot of times, and yeah, some mistakes were of my decisions, and yeah, some mistakes were impressed to be bigger than what actually were. But all in all, I felt like a victim and a hero for myself. I felt alone in every situation, and self-help was the only true way of handling things in my opinion.

In this story based on the life of a God-blessed schizophrenic, things get much better and much worse later on in my life and in the second volume of this book. I achieved success but maintained a stream of downfalls and disappointments. Many illusions and events of trust issues and violence are revealed. Explanations of previous illusions and personal issues became more relevant in further readings contained in the second volume. Neutral individuals, family, friends, organizations, and government entities all have a play in my future, but with my history, knowledge, and understanding of people and situations, I still claim that I am not surely tainted from my own character and actions. Only tainted by what others have planned for me and what others have stereotyped and wanted me to be but failed by my new dedication to God.

Author's Note

I wanted to stop at this point and make a point about this book before continuing with a true story of a God-blessed schizophrenic.

I am acknowledging this date of April 1, 2019—the day after Nipsey Hussle got killed.

He was/is a Crip and a man of greatness.

He used his influence and love of positive power other than himself to better himself and others for greatening the energy of that positive higher power.

I have heard illusions and hallucinations in most artists' music.

I have heard the truth of my situation and knowledge of me in artists' music.

I have always heard my situation and likeness being positive and truthful in his music.

I do believe that he was set up and killed by Zionist Jews, Illuminati, Masons, and legal authorities.

I also believe that I have been set up from my past incidents from my neighborhood childhood and has stemmed into later points in life with a connection of framework and information.

I also want to acknowledge that I have done more crimes that are in this book.

I will not self-incriminate myself by facts and further information.

I have done wrong and received energy of knowledge, techniques, physical and mental strength, and diligence in secrecy and demeanor from my negative activities.

It is said not to be proud of negative activities, but I can appreciate them for what is to come later in my life.

I denounced God before as you read so far in this book. I continue to have turmoil in my life and become more defensive while using violence. I continue to receive blessings and grow more strength in transformation to greatening God with positivity.

Folk was a religion to me, and Crip was an energy that I always saw, worked, cherished, uplifted, held, and loved.

I was a maniac, Latin disciple, Folk gang member, and Crip for most of the time period of this book in both volumes. I am now a former member of both organizations, announced publicly on December 7, 2018.

About the Author

Burgamouth Studios is owned and operated by Robert E. Pace a.k.a. Burgatime Bigbabies a.k.a. Burgatime Da Illest. Burgatime and his production brand have traveled all across the country, recording artists and making his own creations. His preproduction works can be found on www.youtube,com/demonizedmcs, or you can go to YouTube's search pane and type in "Burgamouth Studios." Burgatime is a native of East Cleveland, Ohio, and has been behind the scenes on most music and production scenes, working as an engineer and producer.